ESTATE PUBLIC

CORNWALL

Street Maps of 38 Towns
with index to streets
Road Map with index
Population Gazetteer
Administrative Districts
Postcode Districts

Street plans prepared and published by ESTATE PUBLICATIONS and based upon the ORDNANCE SURVEY maps with the sanction of the controller of H.M. Stationery Office.   Crown copyright reserved

The publishers acknowledge the cooperation of Caradon, Carrick, Kerrier, North Cornwall, Penwith and Restormel District Councils and Cornwall County Council in the preparation of these maps.

ISBN 0 86084 315 7

ESTATE PUBLICATIONS

STREET ATLASES

ASHFORD, TENTERDEN
BASILDON, BRENTWOOD
BASINGSTOKE, ANDOVER
BOURNEMOUTH, POOLE, CHRISTCHURCH
BRIGHTON, LEWES, NEWHAVEN, SEAFORD
BROMLEY (London Borough),
CHELMSFORD, BRAINTREE, MALDON, WITHAM
CHICHESTER, BOGNOR REGIS
COLCHESTER, CLACTON
CRAWLEY & MID SUSSEX
DERBY, HEANOR, CASTLE DONNINGTON
EDINBURGH
EXETER, EXMOUTH
FAREHAM, GOSPORT
FOLKESTONE, DOVER, DEAL
GLOUCESTER, CHELTENHAM
GRAVESEND, DARTFORD
GUILDFORD, WOKING
HASTINGS, EASTBOURNE, HAILSHAM
HIGH WYCOMBE
I. OF WIGHT TOWNS
LEICESTER
MAIDSTONE
MANSFIELD
MEDWAY, GILLINGHAM
NEW FOREST
NOTTINGHAM, EASTWOOD, HUCKNALL, ILKESTON
OXFORD
PLYMOUTH, IVYBRIDGE, SALTASH, TORPOINT
PORTSMOUTH, HAVANT
READING
REIGATE, BANSTEAD, REDHILL
RYE & ROMNEY MARSH
ST. ALBANS, WELWYN, HATFIELD
SALISBURY, AMESBURY, WILTON
SEVENOAKS
SHREWSBURY
SLOUGH, MAIDENHEAD
SOUTHAMPTON, EASTLEIGH
SOUTHEND-ON-SEA
SWALE (Sittingbourne, Faversham, I. of Sheppey)
SWINDON
TELFORD
THANET, CANTERBURY, HERNE BAY, WHITSTABLE
TORBAY
TUNBRIDGE WELLS, TONBRIDGE, CROWBOROUGH
WATFORD, HEMEL HEMPSTEAD
WINCHESTER, NEW ALRESFORD
WORTHING, LITTLEHAMPTON, ARUNDEL

COUNTY ATLASES

AVON
AVON & SOMERSET
BERKSHIRE
CHESHIRE
CORNWALL
DEVON
DORSET
ESSEX
HAMPSHIRE
HERTFORDSHIRE
KENT (64pp)
KENT (128pp)
OXFORDSHIRE
SHROPSHIRE
SOMERSET
SURREY
SUSSEX (64pp)
SUSSEX (128pp)
WILTSHIRE

LEISURE MAPS

SOUTH EAST (1:200,000)
KENT & EAST SUSSEX (1:150,000)
SURREY & SUSSEX (1:150,000)
SOUTHERN ENGLAND (1:200,000)
ISLE OF WIGHT (1:50,000)
WESSEX (1:200,000)
DEVON & CORNWALL (1:200,000)
CORNWALL (1:180,000)
DEVON (1:200,000)
DARTMOOR & SOUTH DEVON COAST (1:100,000)
GREATER LONDON (1:80,000)
EAST ANGLIA (1:250,000)
THAMES & CHILTERNS (1:200,000)
COTSWOLDS & WYEDEAN (1:200,000)
HEART OF ENGLAND (1:250,000)
WALES (1:250,000)
THE SHIRES OF MIDDLE ENGLAND (1:250,000)
SHROPSHIRE, STAFFORDSHIRE (1:200,000)
SNOWDONIA (1:125,000)
YORKSHIRE & HUMBERSIDE (1:250,000)
YORKSHIRE DALES (1:125,000)
NORTH YORK MOORS (1:125,000)
NORTH WEST ENGLAND (1:200,000)
ISLE OF MAN (1:60,000)
NORTH PENNINES & LAKES (1:200,000)
LAKE DISTRICT (1:75,000)
BORDERS OF ENGLAND & SCOTLAND (1:200,000)
BURNS COUNTRY (1:200,000)
ISLE OF ARRAN (1:63,360)
ARGYLL & THE ISLES (1:200,000)
HEART OF SCOTLAND (1:200,000)
GREATER GLASGOW (1:150,000)
LOCH LOMOND & TROSSACHS (1:150,000)
PERTHSHIRE (1:150,000)
FORT WILLIAM, BEN NEVIS, GLEN COE (1:185,000)
IONA (1:10,000) & MULL (1:115,000)
GRAMPIAN HIGHLANDS (1:185,000)
LOCH NESS & INVERNESS (1:150,000)
AVIEMORE & SPEY VALLEY (1:150,000)
SKYE & LOCHALSH (1:130,000)
CAITHNESS & SUTHERLAND (1:185,000)
WESTERN ISLES (1:125,000)
ORKNEY & SHETLAND (1:128,000)
ENGLAND & WALES (1:650,000)
SCOTLAND (1:500,000)
GREAT BRITAIN (1:1,100,000)

ROAD ATLAS

MOTORING IN THE SOUTH (1:200,000)

EUROPEAN LEISURE MAPS

EUROPE (1:3,100,000)
BENELUX (1:600,000)
FRANCE (1:1,000,000)
GERMANY (1:1,000,000)
GREECE & THE AEGEAN (1:1,000,000)
IRELAND (1:625,000)
ITALY (1:1,000,000)
MEDITERRANEAN CRUISING (1:5,000,000)
SCANDINAVEA (1:2,600,000)
SPAIN & PORTUGAL (1:1,000,000)
THE ALPS (1:1,000,000)
THE WORLD (1:35,000,000)
THE WORLD FLAT SHEET

ESTATE PUBLICATIONS are also
sole distributors in the U.K. for:
ORDNANCE SURVEY, Republic of Ireland
ORDNANCE SURVEY, Northern Ireland

Catalogue and prices from ESTATE PUBLICATIONS,
Bridewell House, Tenterden, Kent TN30 6JB.
Tel: 05806 4225   Fax: 05806 3720

CONTENTS

One-way street	⟶	Post Office	●
Pedestrian Precinct	▨	Public Conveniences	Ⓒ
Car Park	🅿	Church	✛

ISLES OF SCILLY

St. Martin's
Bryher
Tresco
Samson
Hugh Town
St. Mary's
Annet
St. Agnes

Diz.
St. Ger

Fire Beacon Pt.
Bosc.
Tintagel Head
Tintagel No
Delabole
St. Teath
Cam

Port Isaac
Pentire Pt.
St. Minver
Gulland Rock
Trevose Head
Padstow
Wadebridge
Park Head
St. Issey
Bodm
A

St. Mawgan
St. Columb Major
Newquay
Restormel
Bugle
Los
Kelsey Head
Penhale Pt.
St. Dennis
W
Perranporth
Newlyn East
St. Blazey
St. Austell
Bawden Rocks
St. Agnes Head
St. Agnes
Carrick
N
Fowey
Porthtowan
Grampound
Gribbin Head
Portreath
Navax Pt.
Godrevy I.
R
Tregony
Black Head
Mevagissey
Truro
Chapel Pt.
St. Ives
St. Day
Redruth
O
Gorran Haven
The Carracks
Gurnard's Head
Camborne
Feock
Veryan
Dodman Pt.
Pendeen Watch
Lelant
Hayle
C
Penryn
Gerrans
Penwith
Ludgvan
Leedstown
Kerrier
Falmouth
St. Mawes
Cape Cornwall
St. Just
Marazion
Zone Pt.
Penzance
St. Michael's Mt.
Mawnan
Rosemullion Head
Newlyn
Helston
LAND'S END
Sennen
St. Buryan
Mousehole
Trewavas Head
Porthleven
Mawgan
Nare Pt.
Gwennap Head
Treen
St. Keverne
Manacle Pt.
Mullion
Coverack
Mullion I.
Black Head
Ruan Minor
Lizard
LIZARD POINT

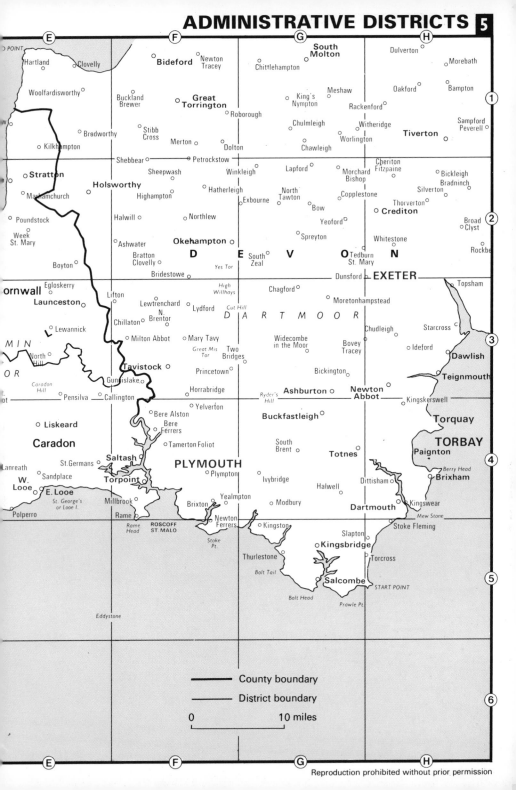

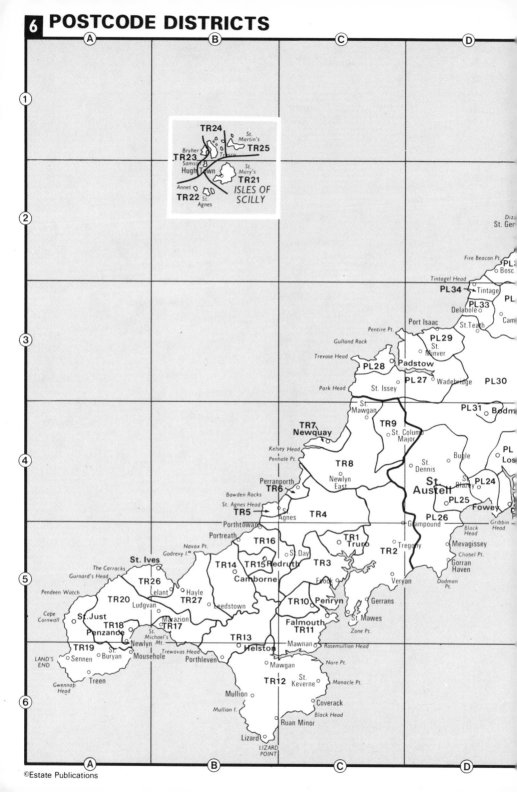

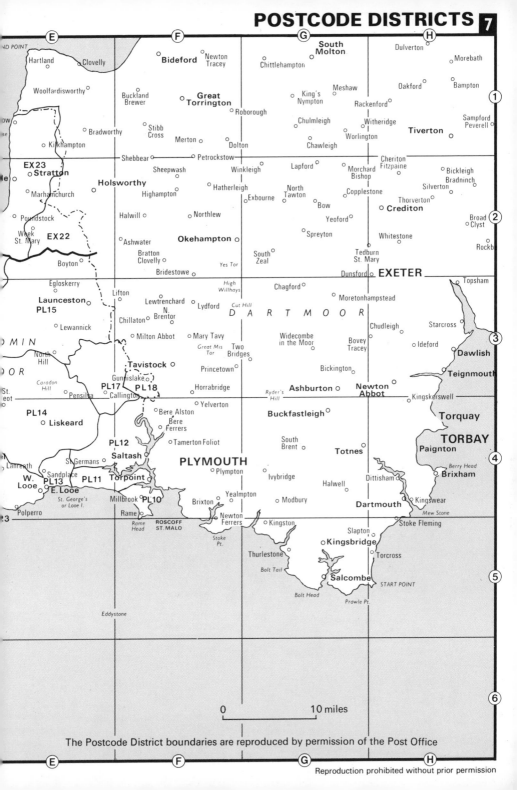

ND POINT
Hartland   Clovelly
Woolfardisworthy
Buckland Brewer
Bideford   Newton Tracey
Chittlehampton
South Molton
Dulverton
Morebath

Meshaw
King's Nympton
Oakford
Bampton

Great Torrington
Roborough
Rackenford

(1)

ow
Bradworthy
Stibb Cross
Merton
Chulmleigh
Witheridge
Worlington
Tiverton

Sampford Peverell

se
Kirkhampton
Shebbear
Petrockstow
Dolton
Chawleigh
Cheriton Fitzpaine

EX23
Stratton
Sheepwash
Winkleigh
Lapford
Morchard Bishop
Bickleigh
Bradninch
Silverton

Marhamchurch
Highampton
Hatherleigh
North Tawton
Copplestone
Thorverton

Poundstock
Halwill
Northlew
Exbourne
Bow
Crediton
Broad Clyst
(2)

Week St. Mary
EX22
Ashwater
Yeoford
Whitestone
Rockb

Boyton
Bratton Clovelly
Bridestowe
Yes Tor
South Zeal
Spreyton
Tedburn St. Mary
Dunsford
EXETER
Topsham

Okehampton

Egloskerry
Lifton
High Willhays
Chagford
Moretonhampstead

Launceston PL15
Lewtrenchard
Lydford
Cut Hill
D A R T M O O R
Chudleigh
Starcross
(3)

N. Brentor
Chillaton
Milton Abbot
Mary Tavy
Widecombe in the Moor
Bovey Tracey
Ideford
Dawlish

OMIN
Lewannick
North Hill
Great Mis Tor
Two Bridges
Princetown
Bickington
Teignmouth

OR
Caradon Hill
Tavistock
Horrabridge
Ryder's Hill
Ashburton
Newton Abbot
Kingskerswell

St. eot
Pensilva
PL17 **PL18**
Callington
Yelverton
Buckfastleigh
Torquay

PL14
Liskeard
Bere Alston
Bere Ferrers
Tamerton Foliot
South Brent
Totnes
TORBAY
Paignton

Lanreath
W. Looe
Sandplace
PL12
Saltash
PLYMOUTH
Plympton
Ivybridge
Halwell
Dittisham
Berry Head
Brixham
(4)

PL13
E. Looe
St. George's or Looe I.
PL11
Torpoint
Millbrook
PL10
Brixton
Yealmpton
Modbury
Dartmouth
Kingswear

Polperro
Rame
Newton Ferrers
Kingston
Stoke Fleming
Mew Stone

3
Rame Head
ROSCOFF ST. MALO
Stoke Pt.
Slapton
(5)

Thurlestone
Bolt Tail
Kingsbridge
Torcross

Bolt Head
Salcombe
START POINT
Prowle Pt.

Eddystone

(6)

0   10 miles

The Postcode District boundaries are reproduced by permission of the Post Office

GAZETTEER INDEX TO ROAD MAP
With populations

County of Cornwall population (including the Isles of Scilly) **432,240**

Districts:
Caradon **68,169**
Carrick **76,629**
Kerrier **83,195**
North Cornwall **66,464**
Penwith **55,691**
Restormel **79,439**

Advent **113**	*
Altarnum **822**	11 E3
Antony **470**	*
Blisland **511**	*
Boconnoc **139**	*
Bodmin, E.C. Wed. **12,269**	10 D4
Boscastle	10 D2
Botus Fleming **648**	*
Boyton **275**	11 E2
Breage **2,661**	10 B5
Broadoak **117**	*
Bryher (Scilly Is.)	10 B1
Bude, E.C. Thurs. (with Stratton)	
6,850	11 E2
Budock **1,100**	10 C5
Bugle	10 D4
Callington, E.C. Thurs.	
2,941	11 E3
Calstock **4,948**	11 F3
Camborne, E.C. Thurs.	
18,504	10 B5
Camelford **1,767**	10 D3
Cardinham **483**	*
Chacewater **1,421**	10 C5
Colan **1,410**	10 C4
Constantine **2,102**	10 C5
Coverack	10 C6
Creed **175**	*
Crowan **1,941**	10 B5
Cubert **828**	10 C4
Cuby **130**	*
Cury **423**	*
Davidstow **394**	*
Delabole	10 D3
Dobwalls **1,654**	*
Duloe **649**	*
East Looe, E.C. Thurs.	
(with W. Looe) **4,509**	11 E4
Egloshayle **340**	*
Egloskerry **279**	11 E3
Falmouth, E.C. Wed. **18,553**	10 C5
Feock **3,252**	10 C5
Forrabury & Minster **806**	*
Fowey, E.C. Wed. **2,535**	10 D4
Germoe **468**	*
Gerrans **1,020**	10 C5
Gorran Haven	10 D5
Grade-Ruan **894**	*
Grampound **435**	10 D5
Gunnislake	11 F3
Gunwalloe **183**	*
Gwennap **1,491**	10 C5
Gwinear-Gwithian **2,286**	10 B5

Hayle, E.C. Thurs. **6,179**	10 B5
Helland **207**	*
Helston, E.C. Wed. **10,809**	10 B6
Hugh Town (Scilly Is.)	10 B2
Isles of Scilly **2,653**	10 B2
Jacobstow **301**	*
Kea **1,592**	10 C5
Kenwyn **3,708**	10 C5
Kilkhampton **896**	11 E1
Ladock **823**	10 C4
Landewednack **811**	*
Landrake with St. Cerney **809**	*
Landulph **411**	*
Laneast **134**	*
Lanhydrock **155**	*
Lanivet **1,371**	*
Lanlivery **429**	*
Lanreath **449**	11 E4
Lansallos **1,621**	11 E4
Lanteglos **1,081**	10 D4
Launcells **421**	*
Launceston, E.C. Thurs.	
6,092	11 E3
Lawhitton Rural **254**	*
Leedstown	10 B5
Lelant	10 B5
Lesnewth **66**	*
Lewannick **588**	11 E3
Lezant **671**	*
Linkinhorne **1,295**	11 E3
Liskeard, E.C. Wed. **6,335**	11 E4
Lizard	10 B6
Lostwithiel, E.C. Wed. **1,998**	10 D4
Ludgvan **2,763**	10 B5
Luxulyan **1,128**	10 D4
Mabe **1,035**	10 C5
Madron **1,269**	10 A5
Manaccan **313**	*
Marazion **1,389**	10 B5
Marhamchurch **475**	11 E2
Mawgan **1,514**	10 B6
Mawnan **1,305**	10 C6
Menheniot **1,287**	11 E4
Mevagissey **2,050**	10 D5
Michaelstow **225**	*
Millbrook **1,780**	11 F4
Morvah **72**	*
Morval **643**	11 E4
Morwenstow **619**	11 E1
Mousehole	10 A6
Mullion **2,109**	10 B6
Mylor Bridge (Mylor **2,400**)	10 C5
Newlyn **1,262**	10 A5
Newlyn East	10 C4
Newquay, E.C. Wed. **16,116**	10 C4
North Hill **763**	11 E3
North Petherwin **564**	*
North Tamerton **270**	*
Otterham **216**	*
Padstow E.C. Wed. **2,806**	10 C3
Paul **214**	*

Pelynt **1,082**	11 E4		St. Mabyn **471**	*	
Penryn, E.C. Thurs. **5,105**	10 C5		St. Martin **542**	*	
Pensilva	11 E3		St. Martin-in-Meneage **278**	*	
Penzance, E.C. Wed. **19,579**	10 A5		St. Martins (Scilly Is.)	10 B1	
Perranarworthal **1,376**	10 C5		St. Mary's (Scilly Is.)	10 B2	
Perranporth	10 C4		St. Mawes	10 C5	
Perranuthnoe **1,554**	10 B5		St. Mawgan **1,213**	10 C4	
Perranzabuloe **4,792**	*		St. Mellion **187**	*	
Philleigh **158**	*		St. Merryn **1,264**	10 C3	
Pillaton **464**	*		St. Mewan **2,651**	10 D4	
Polperro	11 E4		St. Michael Caerhays **95**	*	
Polruan	10 D4		St. Michael Penkevil **204**	*	
Porthleven	10 B6		St. Michael's Mount **26**	10 B5	
Porthtowan	10 B5		St. Minver **2,444**	10 D3	
Port Isaac	10 D3		St. Neot **810**	11 E3	
Portreath	10 B5		St. Pinnock **417**	*	
Poundstock **665**	11 E2		St. Sampson **319**	*	
Probus **1,615**	10 C5		St. Stephen-in-Brannel **4,990**	10 C4	
			St. Stephens (by Launceston) **282**	*	
Quethiock **388**	*		St. Teath **1,730**	10 D3	
			St. Thomas the Apostle **666**	*	
Rame (Maher-with-Rame) **1,104**	11 F4		St. Tudy **458**	*	
Redruth, E.C. Thurs. **28,155**	10 B5		St. Veep **331**	*	
Roche **2,010**	10 D4		St. Wenn **333**	*	
Ruanlaniherne **255**	*		St. Winnow **308**	*	
Ruan Minor	10 C6		Saltash, E.C. Wed. **12,744**	11 F4	
			Sancreed **627**	*	
St. Agnes, E.C. Wed. **5,682**	10 C4		Sandplace	11 E4	
St. Agnes (Scilly Is.)	10 B2		Sennen **772**	10 A6	
St. Allen **309**	*		Sheviock **677**	*	
St. Anthony-in-Meneage **199**	*		Sithney **722**	10 B5	
St. Austell, E.C. Thurs. **34,575**	10 D4		South Hill **415**	*	
St. Blazey	10 D4		South Petherwin **722**	11 E3	
St. Breock **603**	*		Stithians **2,140**	10 C5	
St. Breward **739**	*		Stoke Climsland **1,144**	11 E3	
St. Buryan **998**	10 A6		Stratton, E.C. Thurs (with Bude) **6,850**	11 E2	
St. Cleer **2,566**	11 E4				
St. Clement **799**	*		Tintagel **1,566**	10 D3	
St. Clether **172**	*		Torpoint, E.C. Wed. **8,427**	11 F4	
St. Columb Major, E.C. Wed. **4,073**	10 C4		Towednack **269**	*	
St. Day	10 C5		Treen	10 A6	
St. Dennis, E.C. Wed. **1,987**	10 D4		Tregony **689**	10 C5	
St. Dominick **796**	*		Tremaine **75**	*	
St. Endellion **1,148**	*		Treneglos **94**	*	
St. Enoder **1,420**	10 C4		Tresco (Scilly Is.)	10 B1	
St. Erme **708**	*		Tresmeer **158**	*	
St. Erth **1,040**	*		Trevalga **90**	*	
St. Ervan **373**	*		Trewen **110**	*	
St. Eval **1,155**	*		Truro, E.C. Thurs. **16,348**	10 C5	
St. Ewe **694**	*				
St. Gennys **761**	10 D2		Veryan **880**	10 C5	
St. Germans **2,316**	11 E4				
St. Gluvias **943**	*		Wadebridge, E.C. Wed. **4,009**	10 D3	
St. Goran **1,153**	*		Warbstow **345**	*	
St. Hilary **684**	*		Warleggan **193**	*	
St. Issey **630**	10 C3		Week St. Mary **472**	11 E2	
St. Ive **2,023**	11 E4		Wendron **2,802**	10 B5	
St. Ives, E.C. Thurs. **11,065**	10 B5		Werrington **386**	*	
St. John **229**	*		West Looe, E.C. Thurs. (with E. Looe) **4,509**	11 E4	
St. Juliot **205**	*		Whitstone **397**	*	
St. Just, E.C. Thurs. **4,072**	10 A5		Withiel **305**	*	
St. Just in Roseland **1,120**	*				
St. Keverne **1,874**	10 C6		Zennor **213**	10 A5	
St. Kew **867**	*				
St. Keyne **364**	*				
St. Levan **609**	*				

Population figures are based upon the 1981 census and relate to the local authority area or parish as constituted at that date. Places with no population figure form part of a larger local authority area or parish. District boundaries are shown on pages 4-5 together with population figures.

Population figures in bold type E.C. Early Closing *Parish not shown on map pages 10-11 due to limitation of scale.

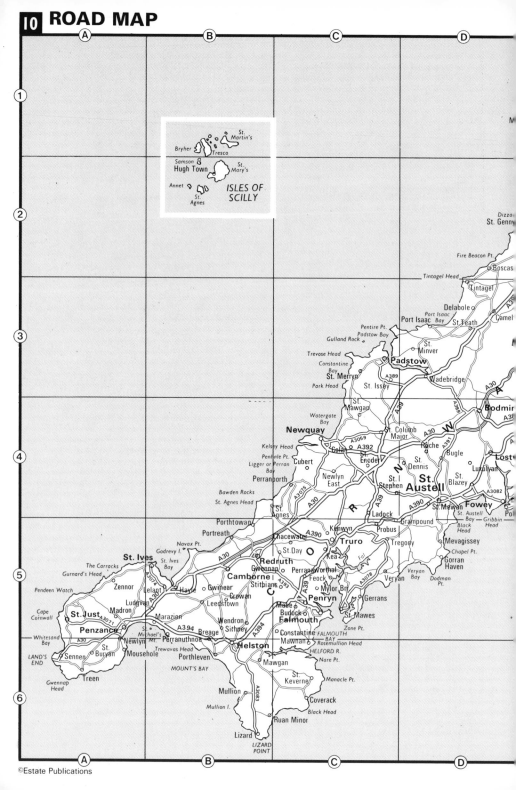

ISLES OF SCILLY

St. Martin's
Bryher
Tresco
Samson
Hugh Town
Annet
St. Agnes
St. Mary's

Dizzo
St. Genn
Fire Beacon Pt.
Boscas
Tintagel Head
Tintagel
Delabole
Port Isaac
Camel
Port Isaac Bay
St. Teath
Pentire Pt.
St. Minver
Padstow Bay
Gulland Rock
Padstow
Trevose Head
Constantine Bay
St. Merryn
Wadebridge
Park Head
St. Issey
Bodmir
A30
St. Mawgan
A38
Watergate Bay
Newquay
St. Columb Major
A3059
W
Kelsey Head
Golan
A392
Roche
Bugle
Penhale Pt.
St. Enoder
St. Dennis
Lost
Ligger or Perran Bay
Cubert
N
Luxulyan
Perranporth
Newlyn East
St. Stephen
St. Austell
St. Blazey
A3082
Bawden Rocks
St. Agnes Head
St. Agnes
A3075
R
Ladock
A390
St. Mewan
Fowey
St. Austell Bay
Gribbin Head
Po
Porthtowan
A30
Kenwyn
Grampound
Black Head
Portreath
A390
Probus
Mevagissey
Chacewater
Truro
Tregony
Chapel Pt.
Navax Pt.
St. Day
Kea
Gorran Haven
Godrevy I.
O
Redruth
The Carracks
St. Ives Bay
Gwennap
Perranworthal
Veryan
Gurnard's Head
Camborne
Feock
Veryan Bay
Dodman Pt.
Pendeen Watch
Zennor
Lelant
Hayle
Stitbians
Mylor Br.
A3078
Gerrans
Cape Cornwall
Ludgvan
Gwinear
Crowan
Mabe
St. Mawes
St. Just
Madron
Leedstown
Budock
Zone Pt.
Whitesand Bay
A3071
Marazion
Wendron
Penryn
Falmouth
Penzance
A394
Breage
Sithney
Constantine
FALMOUTH BAY
LAND'S END
A30
St. Michael's Mt.
Perranuthnoe
Mawnan
Rosemullion Head
Newlyn
St. Buryan
Mousehole
Helston
HELFORD R.
Sennen
Trewavas Head
Porthleven
Mawgan
Nare Pt.
Gwennap Head
Treen
MOUNT'S BAY
St. Keverne
Manacle Pt.
Mullion
Coverack
Mullion I.
A3083
Black Head
Ruan Minor
Lizard
LIZARD POINT

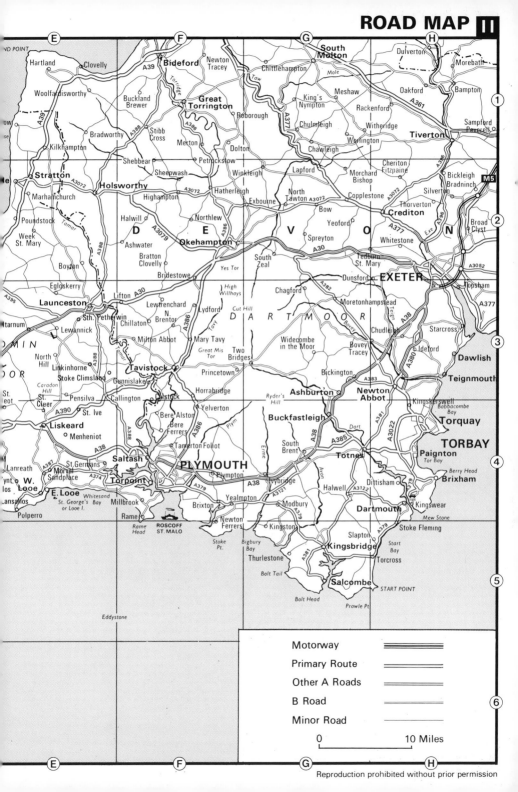

ROAD MAP 11

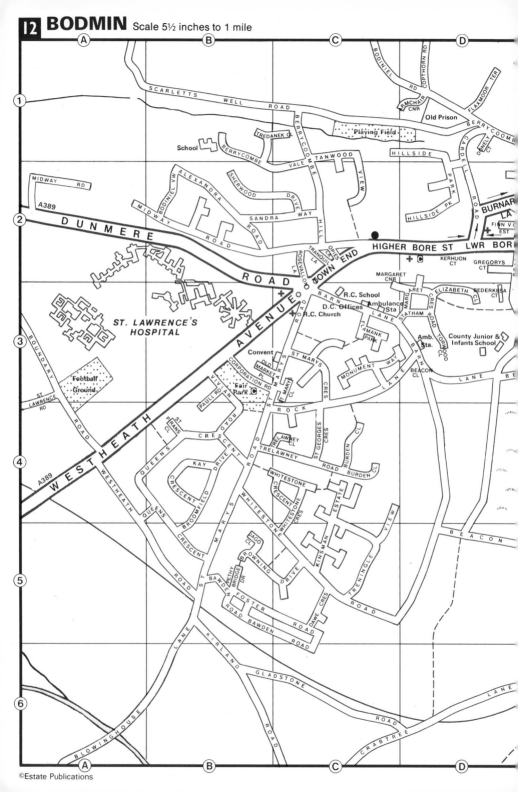

12 BODMIN Scale 5½ inches to 1 mile

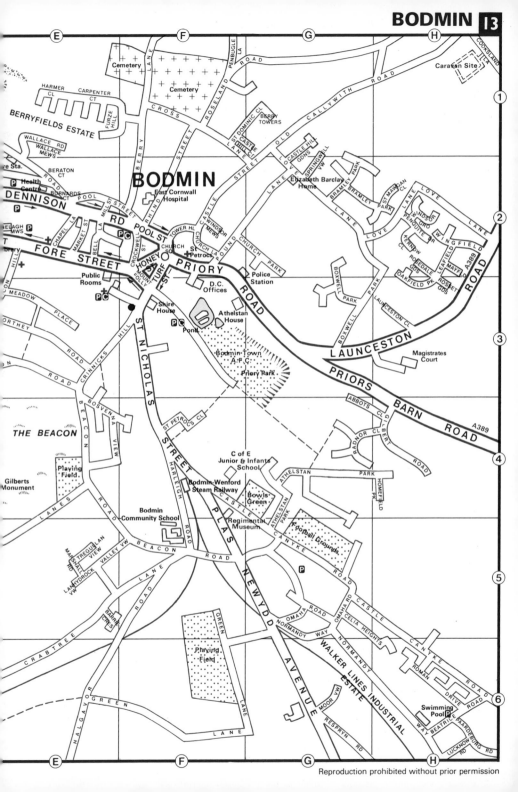

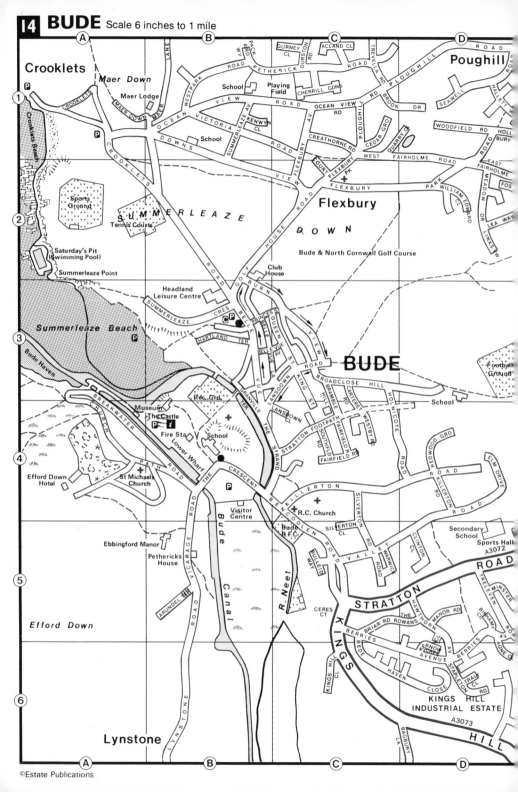

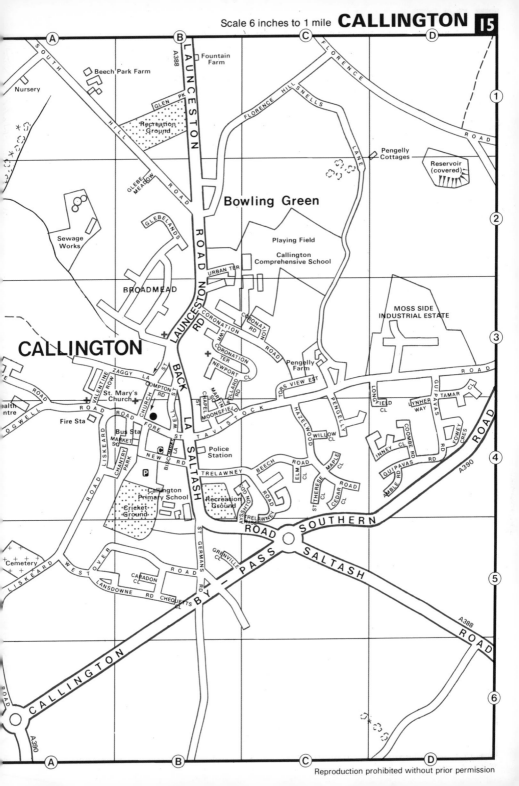

A B C D

1
2
3
4
5
6

Nursery

Beech Park Farm

Fountain Farm

GLEN PK

Recreation Ground

SOUTH

HILL

A388

LAUNCESTON

ROAD

GLEBE MEADOW

Sewage Works

GLEBELANDS

BROADMEAD

URBAN TER

Bowling Green

FLORENCE HILL

SNELLS LANE

FLORENCE ROAD

Pengelly Cottages

Reservoir (covered)

ROAD

Playing Field

Callington Comprehensive School

MOSS SIDE INDUSTRIAL ESTATE

CALLINGTON

ZAGGY LA

VALENTINE ROW

ST

COMPTON S

CHURCH RD

BACK LA

St. Mary's Church

ROAD

Fire Sta

CORONATION

CORONATION RD

CORONATION TER

CORONATION ROAD

NEWPORT CL

Pengelly Farm

TORS VIEW EST

HAZELWOOD

PENGELLY

ROAD

LONG FIELD CL

LYNHER WAY

GUIPAVAS

TAMAR CL

FOWEY CRES

ROAD

MARTINS CHAPEL

MOONSFIEL

DOLLARD RD

WILLOW CL

COOMBE RD

INNEY CL

GUIPAVAS RD

AMBLE RD

A390

Health Centre

DGWELL

ROAD

LISKEARD

ROAD

Bus Sta

MARKET SQ

FORE ST

WELL ST

TAVISTOCK

BEECH ROAD

ELM CL

MAPLE CL

ST THERESE CL

CEDAR CL

ROAD

CHANTRY PARK

NEW RD

BIRCH RD

Police Station

TRELAWNEY

Callington Primary School

Cricket Ground

Recreation Ground

AYSSHTON GDS

TRELAWNE RISE

Cemetery

LISKEARD ROAD

WESTOVER

LANSDOWNE RD

CARADON CL

CHEQUETTS CL

ST GERMANS

ROAD

GRENVILLE CL

BY PASS

ROAD

SOUTHERN

SALTASH

ROAD

A388

ROAD

CALLINGTON

A390

ROAD

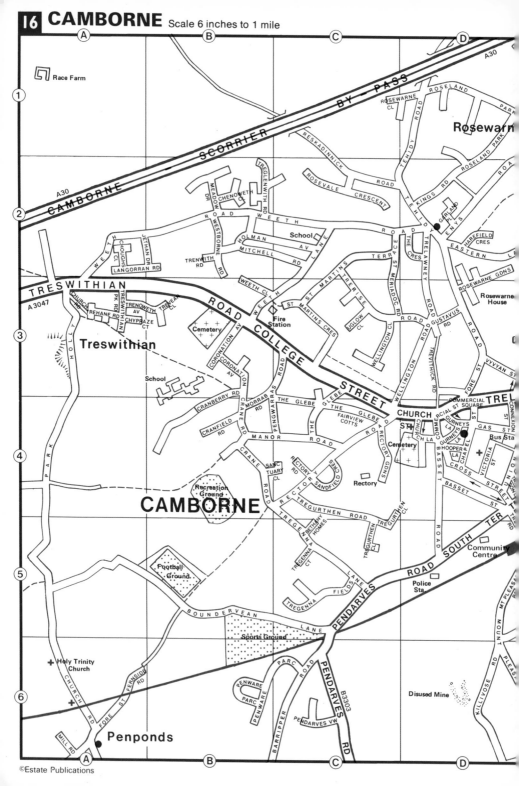

16 CAMBORNE Scale 6 inches to 1 mile

©Estate Publications

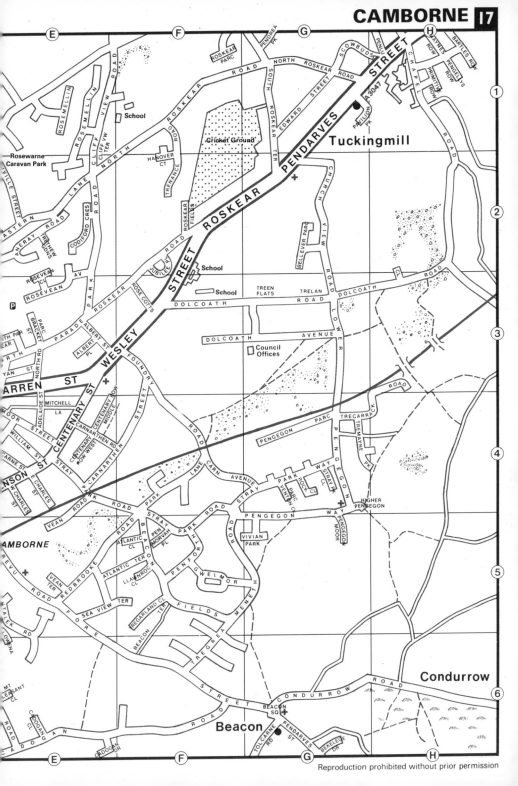

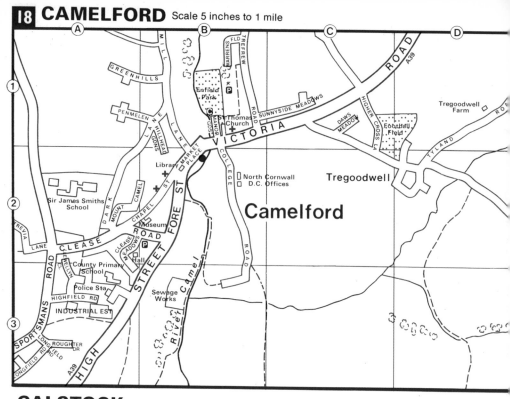

Camelford

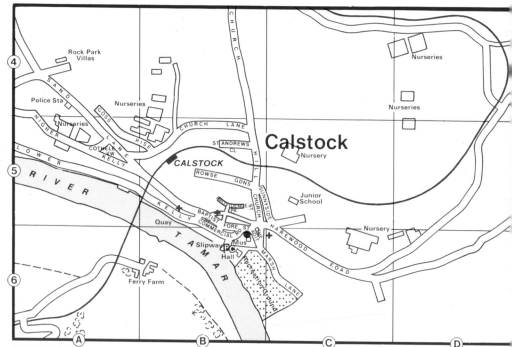

CALSTOCK Scale 6 inches to 1 mile

Calstock

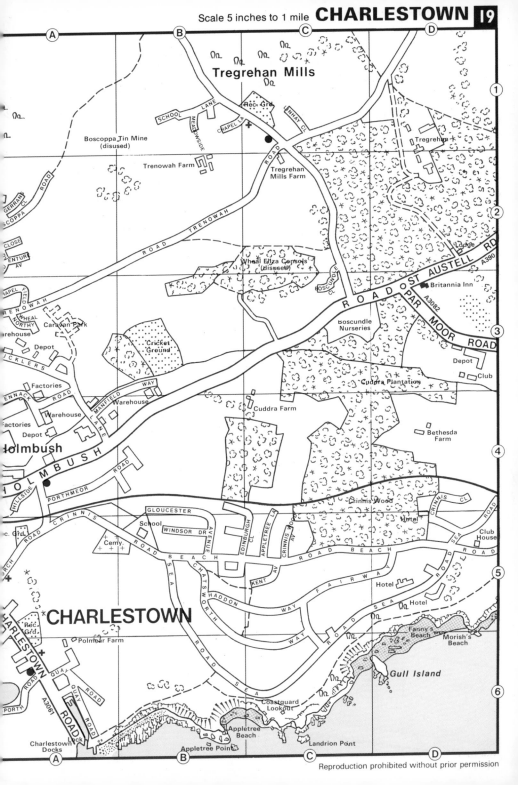

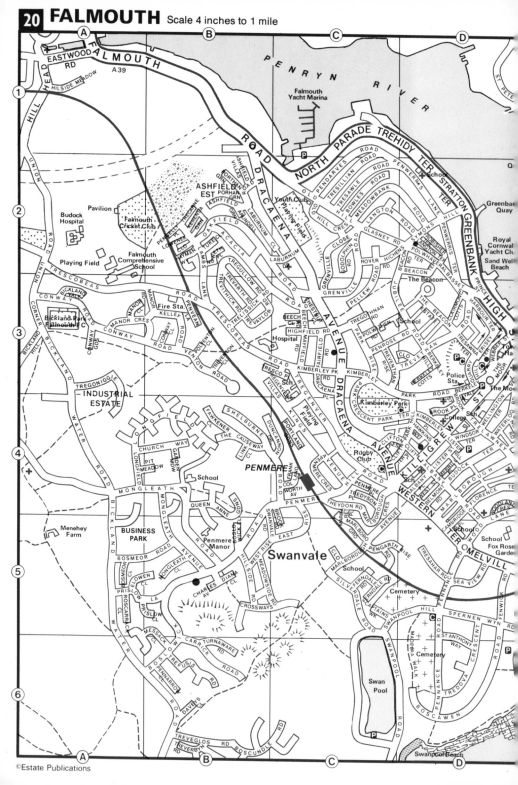

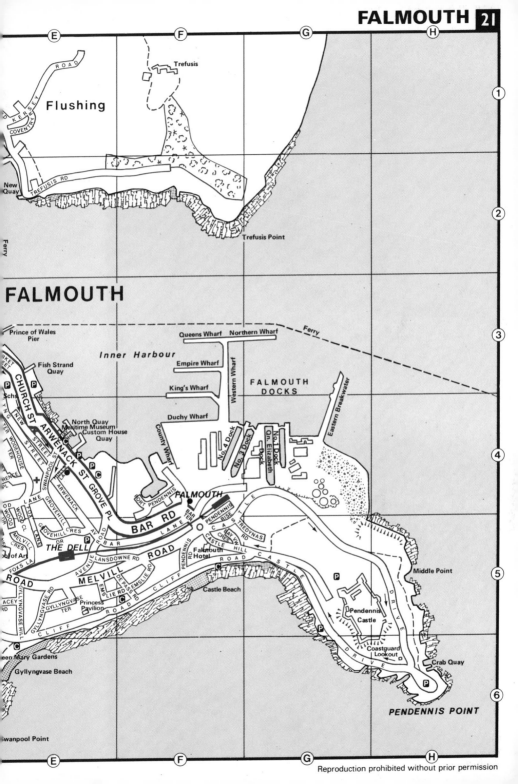

Trefusis

Flushing

ROAD

KERSEY

COVEN

TREFUSIS

New Quay

TREFUSIS RD

Trefusis Point

Ferry

FALMOUTH

Prince of Wales Pier

Fish Strand Quay

Inner Harbour

Queens Wharf   Northern Wharf

Ferry

Empire Wharf

Western Wharf

FALMOUTH DOCKS

King's Wharf

CHURCH ST

ARWENACK ST

NEW STREET

GROVE PL

County Wharf

Duchy Wharf

North Quay
Maritime Museum
Custom House Quay

No 4 Dock

No 3 Dock

Qn. Elizabeth Dock

No 1 Dock

Eastern Breakwater

FALMOUTH

PENDENNIS RISE

BAR RD

ARWENACK

GROVEHILL CRES

SWANPOOL

LANE

THE DELL

LANSDOWNE RD

BAR ROAD

PENDENNIS

CASTLE

TREVONAS

Falmouth Hotel

ROAD

CASTLE HILL

CASTLE

ROAD

MELVILL

GYLLYNGVASE RD

CLIFF RD

EMSLIE RD

PENDENNIS RD

CLIFF

Castle Beach

Middle Point

ROAD

Princess Pavilion

GYLLYNGVASE

CLIFF

Pendennis Castle

DRIVE

FOXS LA

ol of Ar

Queen Mary Gardens

Gyllyngvase Beach

Coastguard Lookout

DRIVE

Crab Quay

Swanpool Point

PENDENNIS POINT

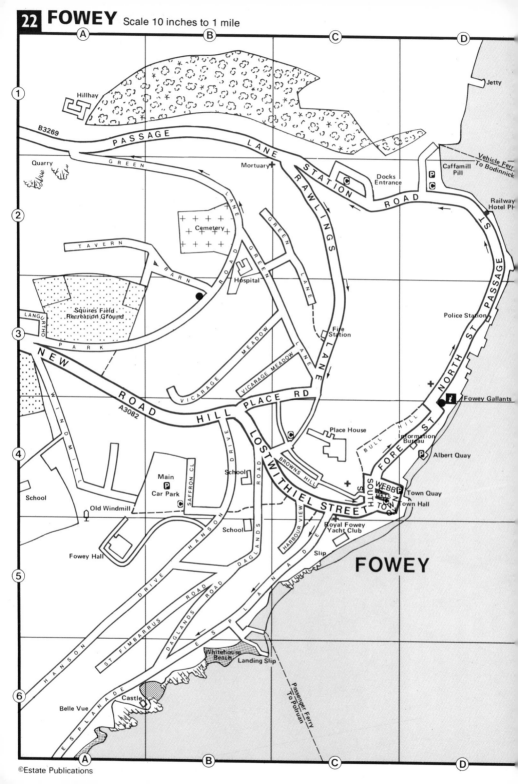

FOWEY

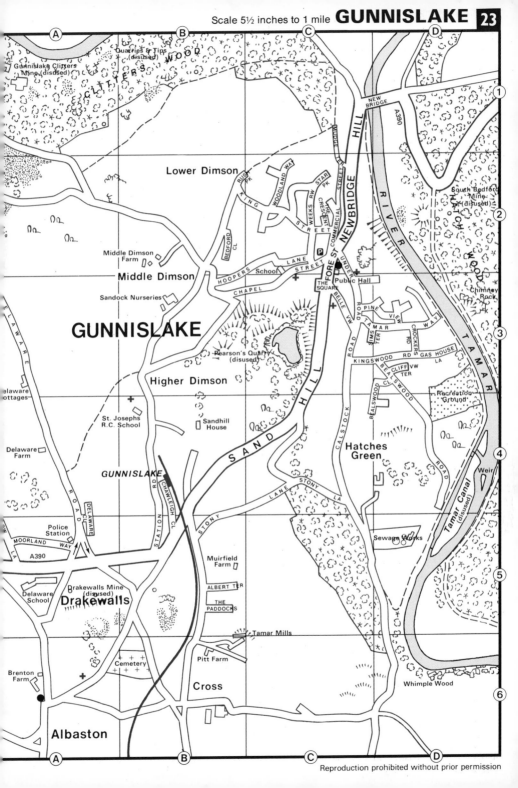

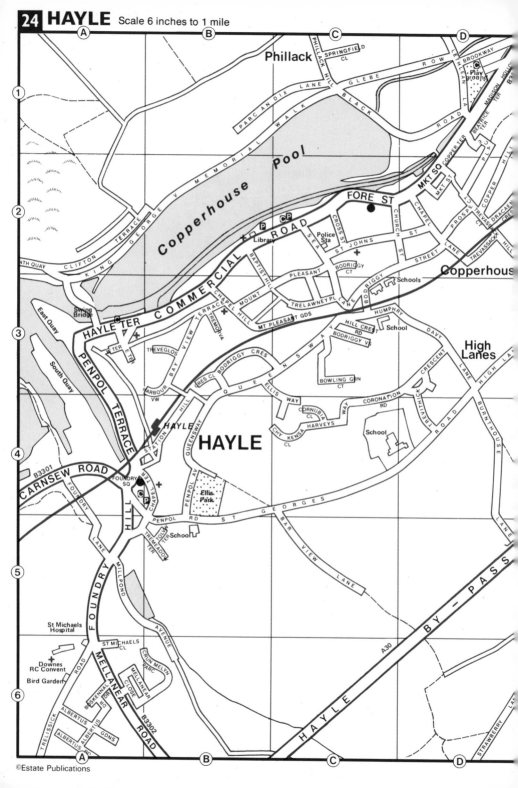

24 HAYLE   Scale 6 inches to 1 mile

Phillack

Copperhouse Pool

FORE ST

MKT SQ

Copperhous

COMMERCIAL ROAD

Library

Police Sta

St JOHNS

BODRIGGY CT

Schools

Pleasant

TRELAWNEY PL

MT PLEASANT GDS

HUMPHRY

HILL CREST RD

School

BODRIGGY VF

High Lanes

BAY VIEW TERRACE

TREMORVA

TREVEGLOS

BODRIGGY CRES

CRES CL

QUEENS WAY

ELLIS WAY

WAY

CORONATION RD

BOWLING GRN CT

School

HARBOUR VW

HAYLE

HAYLE

STATION HILL

QUEENSWAY

PENPOL AV

CORNUBIA CL

CHY KENSA CL

HARVEYS

School

East Quay

South Quay

Swing Bridge

PENPOL TERRACE

HAYLE TER

WATER LANE

CARNSEW ROAD

B3301

FOUNDRY

FOUNDRY SQ

CHAPEL HILL

PENPOL RD

Ellis. Park

ST GEORGES

BAR VIEW LANE

BY - PASS

TREMEADOW

School

A30

HAYLE

HILL

FOUNDRY LANE

MILLPOND

St Michaels Hospital

ST MICHAELS CL

AVENUE

CRIN MELYN PARC

MELLANEAR CLOSE

TREVITHICK LANE

DAVY LANE

CRESCENT

BODRIGGY LANE

CROSS ST

SEA LANE

BAPTIST HILL

CHAPEL HILL

MOUNT

GEORGE V MEMORIAL WALK

KING TERRACE

CLIFTON TERRACE

NTH QUAY

PARC AN DIX LANE

PHILLACK HILL

SPRINGFIEL CL

GLEBE

BLACK

ROW

LETHEAN LA

BROOKWAY

Play groung

MADISON TER

HOLO

BEATRICE TER

COPPER TER

COPPER

PROSPER

DRACAE

CRE

TREVASSACK HILL

CHAPEL ST

STREET

CHURCH ST

MKT ST

MAT ST

Downes RC Convent

Bird Garden

ST MICHAELS ROAD

MELLANEAR ROAD

B3302

BESKENNA SQ

TRELISSICK RD

ALBERTUS TOR

ALBERTUS GDNS

ALBERTUS

BURNTHOUSE LANE

HIGH LANE

©Estate Publications

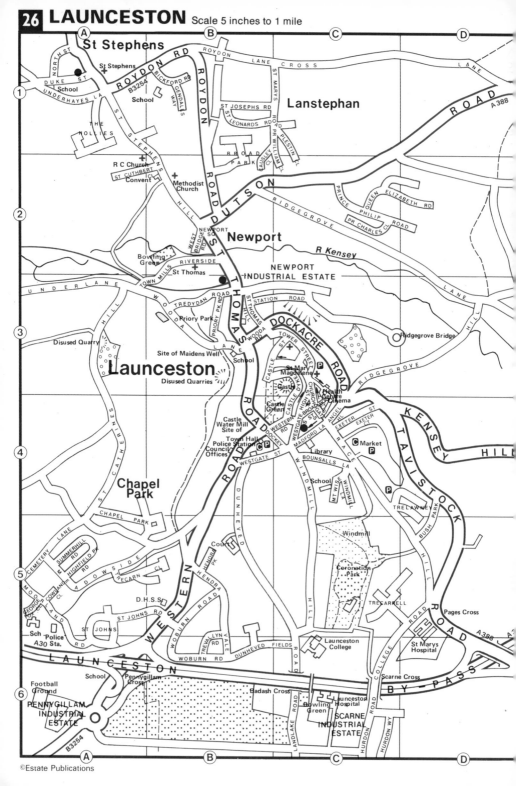

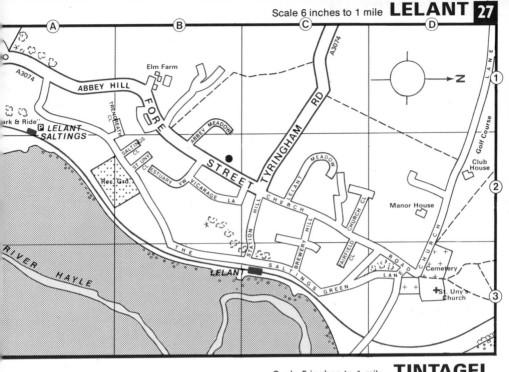

A3074
ABBEY HILL
Elm Farm
FORE
STREET
P LELANT SALTINGS
Park & Ride
TRENEATH CL
SALTINGS CL
ST UNY CL
ESTUARY VW
ABBEY MEADOW
VICARAGE LA
Rec. Grd.
RIVER HAYLE
THE SALTINGS
STATION HILL
CHURCH HILL
BREWERY HILL
TYRINGHAM RD
A3074
MEADOW
LELANT
CHURCH CL
FAIRFIELD CL
SALTINGS GREEN
LELANT
ROAD
CHURCH LANE
Manor House
Cemetery
+ + St. Uny's Church
Golf Course
Club House
N → Z
①
②
③

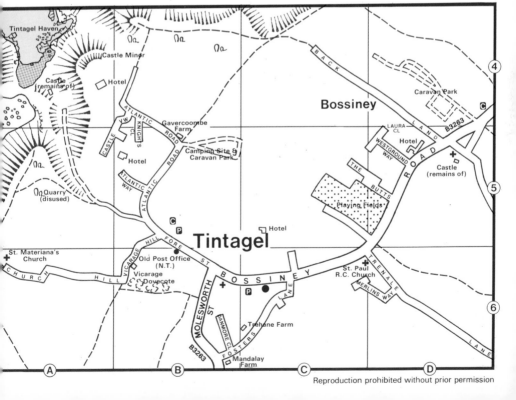

Tintagel Haven
Castle Miner
Castle (remains of)
Hotel
ATLANTIC ROAD
CASTLE VW
KNIGHTS
Gavercoombe Farm
Camping Site & Caravan Park
Hotel
ATLANTIC WAY
ATLANTIC
Quarry (disused)
St. Materiana's Church
CHURCH HILL
VICARAGE HILL
FORE ST
P
C
Tintagel
Old Post Office (N.T.)
Vicarage
Dovecote
P
MOLESWORTH ST
TANMORE CLOSTERS
B3263
Mandalay Farm
Trehane Farm
BOSSINEY LANE
Hotel
BACK LANE
Bossiney
LAURA CL
Hotel
WESTGROUND WAY
THE BUTTS
Playing Fields
B3263
ROAD
Castle (remains of)
St. Paul R.C. Church
TRENALE LANE
MERLINS WAY
Caravan Park
C
④
⑤
⑥

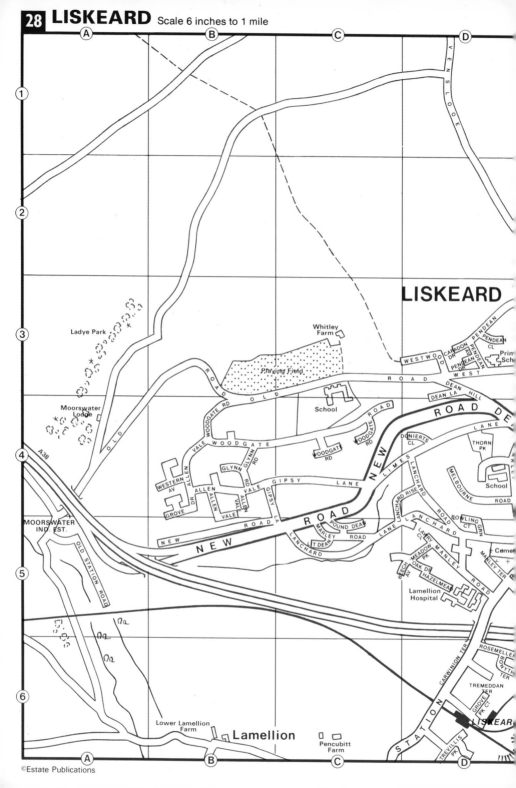

28 LISKEARD   Scale 6 inches to 1 mile

LISKEARD

Ladye Park

Whitley Farm

Moorswater Lodge

WESTWOOD ROAD

PENDEAN
PENDEAN
CL
CARADON DR
PENDEAN
PENDEAN
WEST
Prim
Sch

Playing Field

OLD ROAD

ROAD

DEAN HILL
DEAN LA
ROAD DEAN

School

WOODGATE RD

OLD ROAD

WOODGATE RD

WOODGATE RD

WOODGATE ROAD

LANE

THORN PK

MELBOURNE ROAD

DONIERTS CL

A38

WESTERN AV
ALLEN DR
GLYNN RD
VALE
GIPSY LANE
GIPSY VALE
GLYNN RD
VALE
ALLEN
ALLEN VALE
GROVE

LIMES

NEW ROAD

LANCHARD ROAD

School

BOWLING GRN

Moorswater IND. EST.

OLD STATION ROAD

NEW ROAD

NEW ROAD
LANCHARD

T DEAN

POUND DEAN
MARLEY ROAD

LANCHARD LANE
LANCHARD RISE

LANEY CT

MANLEY ROAD

Cemet

MARLEY TER

BEECH
MEADOW PK
OAK DR
HAZELMEAD

Lamellion Hospital

ROSEMELLEN
BOYNTH
TER

CARWINION TER

STATION

TREMEDDAN TER

GROVE
PK CT

LISKEARD

TREVILLIS PK

Lower Lamellion Farm

Lamellion

Pencubitt Farm

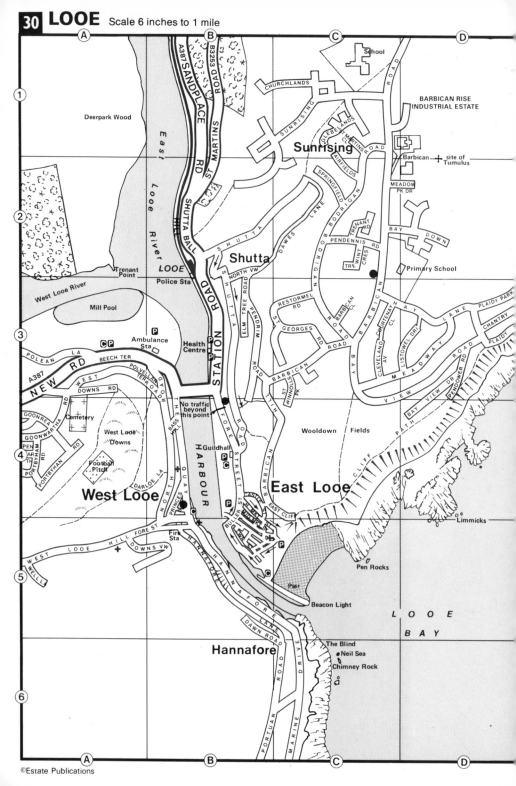

30 LOOE Scale 6 inches to 1 mile

A B C D

1

Deerpark Wood

BARBICAN RISE
INDUSTRIAL ESTATE

CHURCHLANDS

SUNRISING

Sunrising

CLEBELANDS
ST MARTINS ROAD
AIRFIELDS

School

ROAD

Barbican

site of Tumulus

East Looe River

A387 SANDPLACE RD
ST MARTINS ROAD
B3253

SPRINGFIELD
DAWES LANE

BODRIGAN

MEADOW PK DR

TRENANT RD

BAY DOWN

2

Trenant Point

LOOE

Police Sta

SHUTTA BALL

NORTH VW

SHUTTA

Shutta

PENDENNIS RD
TRE
WINT CRES

BODRIGAN ROAD

BAY

Primary School

West Looe River

Mill Pool

3

Ambulance Sta

Health Centre

STATION ROAD

ELM TREE ROAD

PENDRIM

RESTORMEL RD

ST GEORGES

BARBICAN CL

CLEVELAND AV
COURTENAY
CL
LISTOWEL DRI

HAY
MEADWAY

PLAIDY PARK
CHANTRY
PLAIDY

POLEAN LA
A387 NEW RD

CP

BEECH TER

POLVELLAN TERRACE
WEST DOWNS RD

ROAD

BARBICAN PK
ST WINNOLLS
HILL ROAD

BARBICAN ROAD

BAY VIEW
PENDOWER RD
BAY VIEW DR

ROAD

4

GOONREA
GOONWARTHA RD
PEN PARK
PORTBYHAN RD

Cemetery

West Looe Downs

Football Pitch

DARLOE LA

THE QUAY
BASS HILL
NORTH

No traffic beyond this point

Guildhall

HARBOUR

FORE STREET

Wooldown   Fields

East Looe

CLIFF PATH

Limmicks

West Looe

P

P
P

EAST CLIFF
BULLER ST

Pen Rocks

LOOE
WELL
LOOE HILL
FORE ST
DOWNS VW

5

PRINCES
Fire Sta

HANNAFORE LANE

Pier

Beacon Light

L O O E   B A Y

DAWN ROAD

Hannafore

The Blind
Neil Sea
Chimney Rock

PORTUAN ROAD
MARINE DRIVE

6

A B C D

©Estate Publications

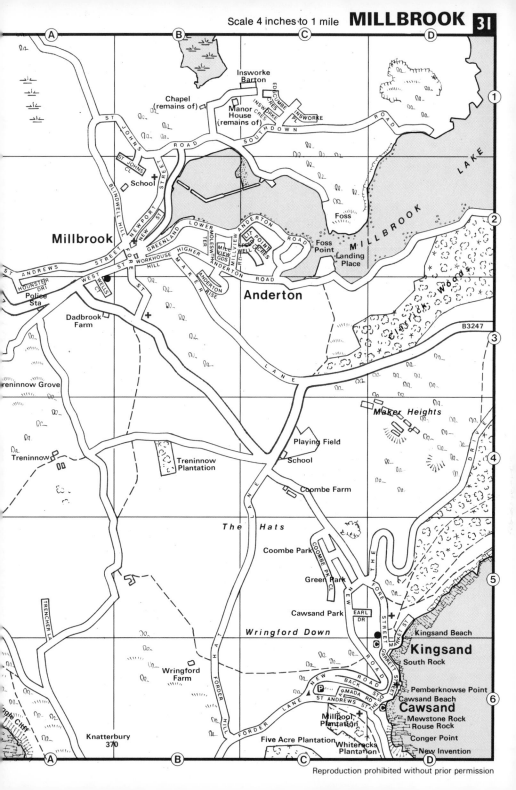

Insworke Barton

Chapel (remains of)

Manor House (remains of)

Insworke

ST JOHNS

EDGCUMBE CRES

INSWORKE

INSWORKE RD

SOUTHDOWN

ST JOHNS CL

School

ROAD

MILLBROOK LAKE

Millbrook

NEWPORT ST

NEW ST

ST STREET

GREENLAND

LOWER MOLESWORTH TER

HIGHER ANDERTON

ANDERTON

ANDERTON RISE

MILLVIEW RD

LIT POINT

CREST ACRES

WELL

MILL VIEW GDS

Foss

Foss Point

Landing Place

M I L L B R O O K

ST ANDREWS

WEST ST

FORD ST

WELLS CL

WORKHOUSE HILL

ANDERTON ROAD

Anderton

C L A C K   W O O D S

HOUNSTER DRI

Police Sta

Dadbrook Farm

B3247

Treninnow Grove

M A K E R

L A N E

Maker Heights

Treninnow

Treninnow Plantation

Playing Field

School

THE DRIVE

Coombe Farm

The Hats

L A N E

Coombe Park

COOMBE PK CL

NEW ROAD

THE FORE STREET

TRENCHER LA

Green Park

Cawsand Park

EARL DR

Kingsand Beach

GARRETT STREET

Kingsand

South Rock

Wringford Down

H A T T

F O R D E R   H I L L

MADA

P

ST ANDREWS

BACK SOUTH

NEW ROAD

Pemberknowse Point

Cawsand Beach

Cawsand

Wringford Farm

Knatterbury 370

F O R D E R   L A N E

Millpool Plantation

Five Acre Plantation

Whiterocks Plantation

Mewstone Rock

Rouse Rock

Conger Point

New Invention

le Cliff

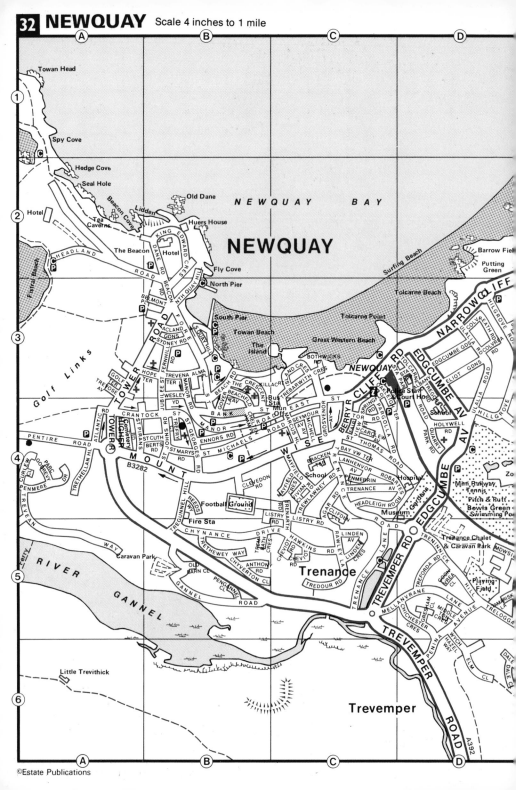

A   B   C   D

1
2
3
4
5
6

Towan Head
Spy Cove
Hedge Cove
Seal Hole
Old Dane
Beacon Cove
Lidden
Hotel
Tea Caverns
Huers House

N E W Q U A Y   B A Y

NEWQUAY

The Beacon
Hotel
Fly Cove
North Pier
Surfing Beach
Barrow Fields
Putting Green
Tolcarne Beach

HEADLAND ROAD
Fistral Beach
BELMONT
KING EDWARD CRES
DANE RD
BEACON RD
NTH QUAY HILL

South Pier
Towan Beach
The Island
Great Western Beach
Tolcarne Point

NEWQUAY
NARROW CLIFF
CLIFF RD
EDGCUMBE AV
EDGCUMBE GDNS
ELIOT GDNS
COLVREATH RD
COLVEAN RD
HILGROVE RD
COLREATH RD
ULALIA ROAD
HILLGROVE

Golf Links

ACLAND GDNS
SYDNEY RD
HOPE TER
TREVENA TER
FERNHILL
JUBILEE ST
WESLEY
MANOR RD
ALMA
BEACHFIELD AV
THE CRESCENT
KILLACOURT
TREBARWITH CRES
BANK
ST GEORGES RD
MOUNT WISE
ST THOMAS
FORE ST
Court Hotel
Police Sta
SCHOOL
HOLYWELL
QUARRY
PARK AV

TOWER RD
TOWER HILL
TREGEMBO AV
ATLANTIC RD
CRANTOCK ST
ST CUTH
ST PIRANS
ST BERTS RD
ST MARYS RD
ST MICHAELS RD
ENNORS RD
CLEVEDON RD

PENTIRE ROAD
CURLEW
PARC GODREY
PENMERE
TRETHELLAN HL
TREVEAN
M O U N T   B3282

MAYFIELD RD
TREVARTH
LISTRY RD
LISTRY RD
School
BRACKEN
LANHENVOR AV
PENMERRIN
TRENANCE AV
SEYMOUR AV
MICHELL AV
GROSVENOR AV
BAY VW TER
ST THOMAS ROAD
ROBARTES RD
HEADLEIGH ROAD
Hospital
Museum
Carthew
TRENINNICK
TREFORDA

Football Ground
Fire Sta
CHYNANCE
RETHEWEY WAY
CHYVERTON CL
ANTHONY RD
PENGANNEL CL
OLD BARN CL
GANNEL ROAD
TREWARTHA
DRIVE
HAWKINS
CHEV
LINDEN AV
RAWLEY LA
CLIFTON
AGAR RD
LINDEN CRES

WAY
Caravan Park

R I V E R   G A N N E L

Trenance
TREDOUR RD
TREDOUR RD
MELLANVRANE LANE
CHICHESTER CRES
GREEN
MIDDLE AVENUE
TRELOGGA
PENINA WAY
HAZEL CL
DALE RD
WICH WAY
ELM CL

TREVEMPER RD
TREVEMPER ROAD
A392

Little Trevithick

Trevemper

Min Railway, Tennis
Pitch & Putt
Bowls Green
Swimming Pool
Zo
Trenance Chalet
& Caravan Park
Playing Field
Trenance

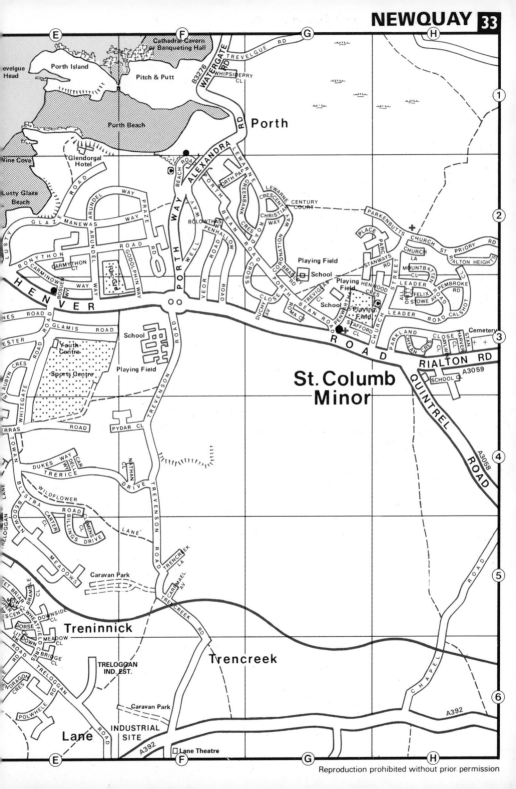

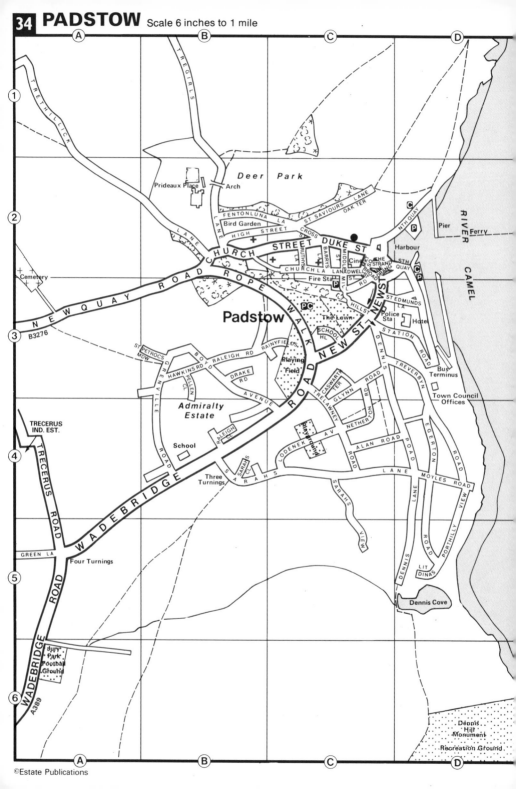

TREGIRLS

TRETHILLICK

Deer Park

Prideaux Place   Arch

FENTONLUNA LA

ST SAVIOURS LANE   OAK TER

Bird Garden   CROSS ST   NTH QUAY   Pier

HIGH STREET

CHURCH   STREET   DUKE ST   Harbour

LANE   SPRUTHYS LA   BARRYS LA   MIDDLE ST   THE STRAND   STH QUAY

Cemetery   CHURCH LA   LANADWELL ST   BROADWAY

NEWQUAY   ROAD   ROPE   Fire Sta   MILL RD   HILLST   ST EDMUNDS LA

B3276   Cine   Police Sta   Hotel

PC   The Lewn   STATION   ROAD

SCHOOL   HL   Bus Terminus

ST PETROCS MDW   RAINYFIELDS   NEW   ST   DENNIS   ROAD   Town Council Offices

GRENVILLE   HAWKINS RD   BOYD   RALEIGH RD   Playing Field   CASWARTH TER   TREVERBYN   ROAD   EGERTON   ROAD

DRAKE RD   AVENUE   TRELAWNEY TER   GLYNN RD   NETHERTON RD   MOYLES ROAD   PORTHILLY VIEW

Padstow

Admiralty Estate

School   RALEIGH CL   LODENEK AV   Playground   ALAN ROAD   LANE   DENNIS ROAD   LIT DINAS

ROAD   SARAHS CL   SARAHS   Three Turnings   SARAH'S   LANE   SARAH'S VIEW

TRECERUS IND. EST.

TRECERUS   ROAD   WADEBRIDGE   ROAD

GREEN LA   Four Turnings

WADEBRIDGE   ROAD

A389

Jubly Park Football Ground

Dennis Cove

RIVER   CAMEL   Ferry

Dennis Hill Monument   Recreation Ground

©Estate Publications

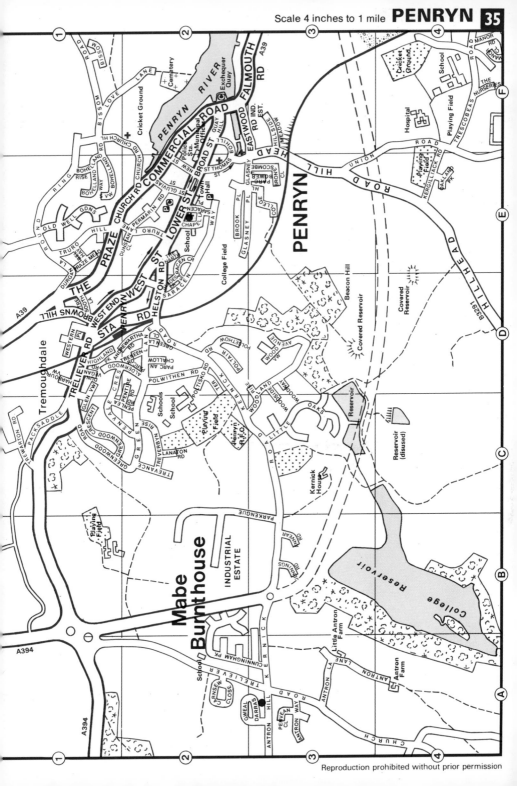

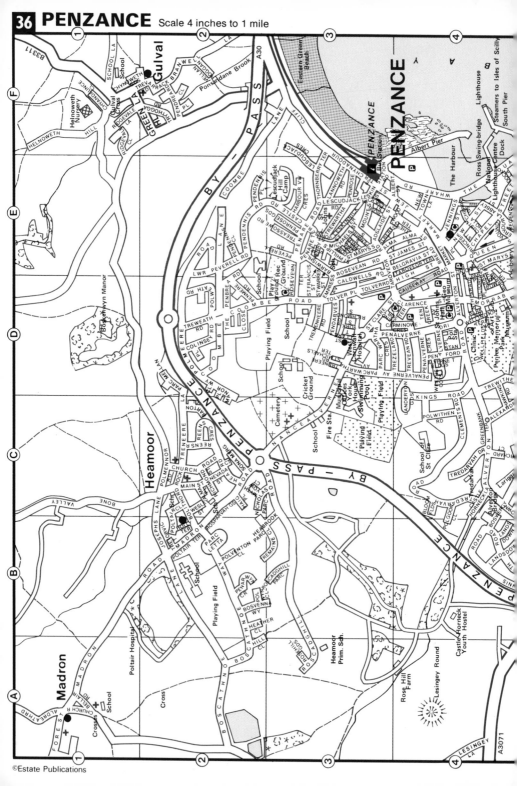

PENZANCE
Scale 4 inches to 1 mile

©Estate Publications

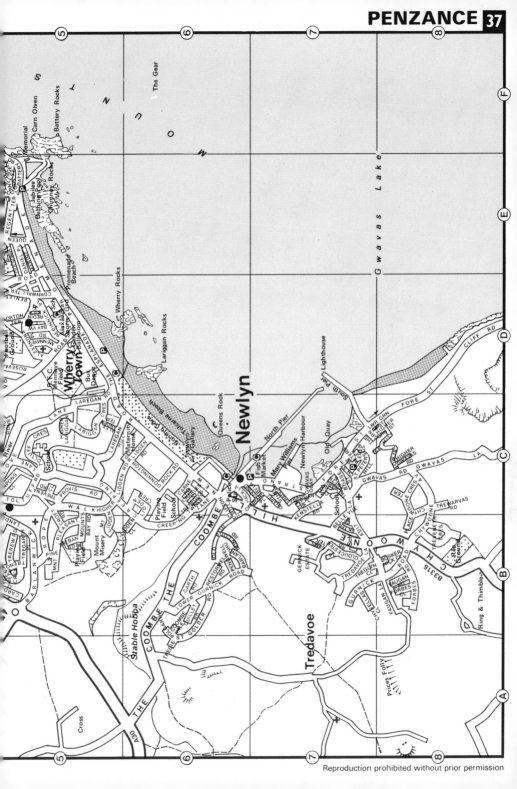

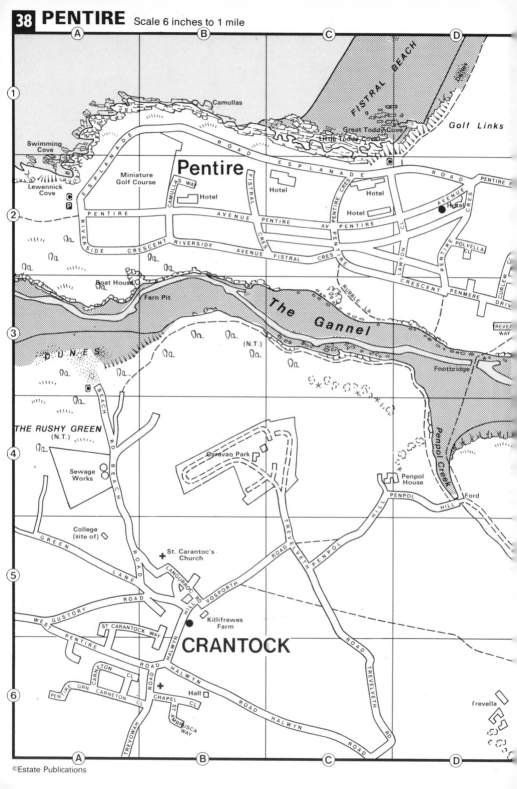

FISTRAL BEACH

Camullas

Golf Links

Great Toddy Cove
Little Toddy Cove

Swimming
Cove

ESPLANADE ROAD

Pentire

ROAD

ESPLANADE

Lewennick
Cove

Miniature
Golf Course

CAMULLAS WAY

Hotel

Hotel

Hotel

Hotel

Hotel

PENTIRE CRES

PENTIRE AVENUE CRES

AVENUE PENTIRE

PENTIRE AV

FISTRAL

PENTIRE RIVERSIDE CRESCENT

RIVERSIDE AVENUE FISTRAL CRES

PENTIRE

LAWTON CL

AVENUE

CRESCENT PENMERE

PENTIRE CRES

POLVELLA CL

CURLEW

DRIV

BUBBLE LA

The Gannel

REVEA
WAY

Boat House

Fern Pit

DUNES

(N.T.)

Footbridge

BEACH RD

Penpol Creek

THE RUSHY GREEN
(N.T.)

Sewage
Works

Caravan Park

Penpol
House

Ford

BEACH ROAD

PENPOL HILL

PENPOL HILL

College
(site of)

GREEN

St. Carantoc's
Church

TREVEVTH ROAD

PENPOL

ROAD

LANGURROC RD

VOSPORTH

HILL

LANE

Killifrewes
Farm

WES GUSTORY

GREEN ROAD

ST CARANTOCK WAY

CRANTOCK

ROAD

HALWYN ROAD

TREVELVETH RD

PENTIRE

CARNETON CL

CARNETON CL

PEN RE GRN

CHAPEL ST

ROAD

Hall

HALWYN ROAD

ROAD HALWYN ROAD

Trevella

TREVOWAH

TMBRUSCA WAY

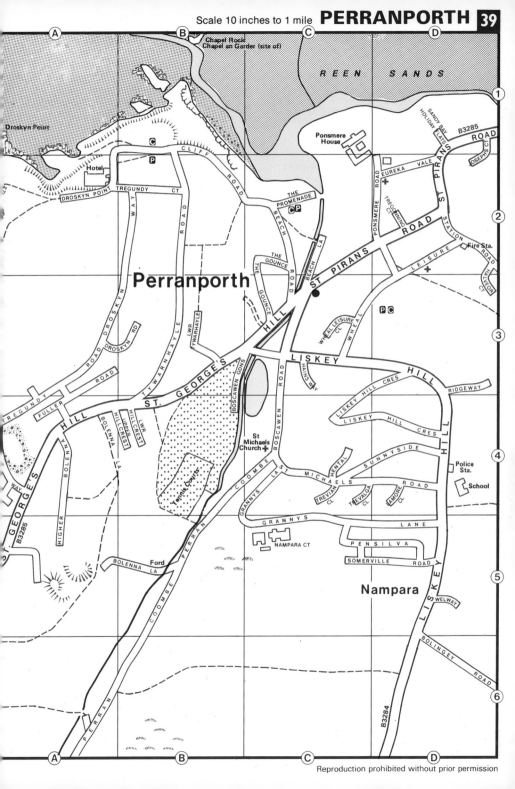

Perranporth

Nampara

Droskyn Point

Chapel Rock
Chapel an Garder (site of)

REEN SANDS

Ponsmere House

Hotel

B3285

JOSEPHS CT

SANDY BAY HOLIDAY FLATS

ST PIRANS ROAD

EUREKA VALE

PONSMERE ROAD

TRECONNING ROAD

STATION ROAD

Fire Sta.

HALVEOR

LEISURE

CLIFF ROAD

TREGUNDY CT

THE PROMENADE
C P

THE GOUNCE ROAD
THE GOUNCE ROAD

BEACH LA

ST PIRANS HILL

BEACH RD

WHEAL LEISURE CL

WHEAL

P C

LISKEY HILL

HAINS WAY

RIDGEWAY

LISKEY HILL CRES

LISKEY HILL CRES

DROSKYN POINT

WAY

DROSKYN ROAD

TYWARNHAYLE RD

LWR TYWARNHAYLE

ST. GEORGES HILL

BOSCAWEN GDNS

BOSCAWEN ROAD

St Michaels Church

MICHAELS

SUNNYSIDE

LISKEY HILL

Police Sta.

School

TREGUNDY

FULLER

BOLENNA

LWR HILLCREST

UPPER HILLCREST

HILLCREST LA

Tennis Courts

COOMBE

GRANNYS LA

TREVIAN CL

TREVALGA CL

AMORE CL

ROAD

ST. GEORGES HILL

WAY

B3285

HIGHER

BOLENNA

BOLENNA LA

Ford

COOMBE PERRAN

GRANNYS

LANE

PENSILVA

SOMERVILLE ROAD

NAMPARA CT

WELWAY

LISKEY HILL

BOLINGEY ROAD

PERRAN

B3284

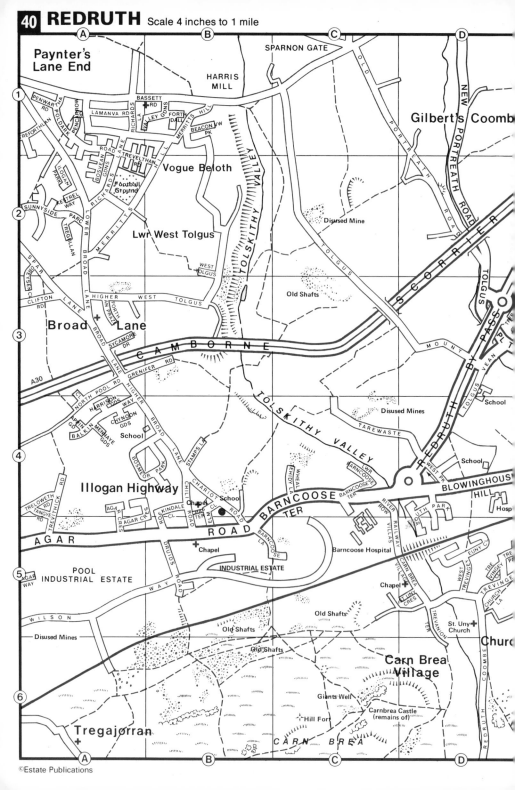

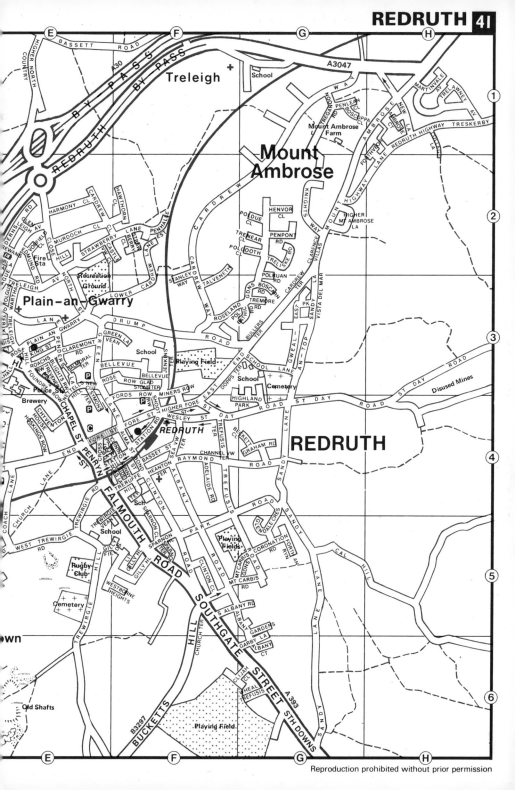

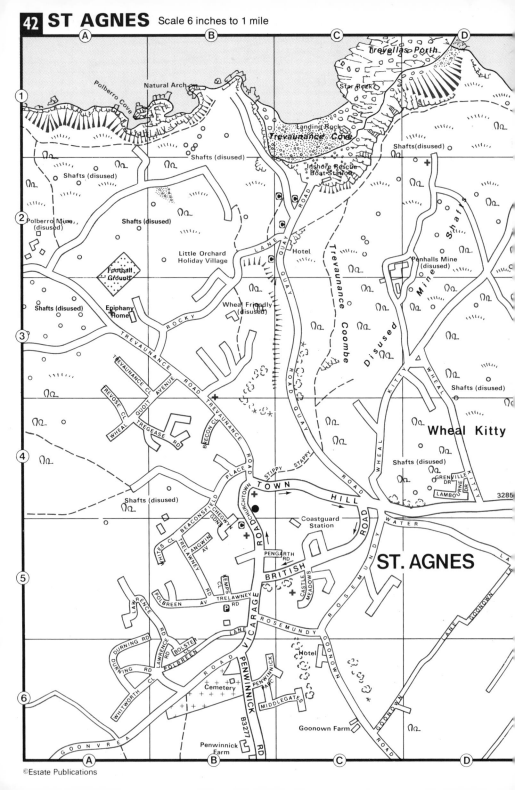

Trevellas Porth

Polberro Cove

Natural Arch

Star Rock

Landing Rock

Trevaunance Cove

Shafts (disused)

Shafts (disused)

Shafts (disused)

Inshore Rescue
Boat Station

Polberro Mine
(disused)

Shafts (disused)

Penhalls Mine
(disused)

Hotel

Little Orchard
Holiday Village

Football
Ground

Epiphany
Home

Shafts (disused)

Wheal Friendly
(disused)

Trevaunance Coombe

Disused Kitty Mine Shaft

Wheal Kitty

Shafts (disused)

Shafts (disused)

TREVAUNANCE ROAD

TREVAUNANCE AVENUE

ROCKY

QUOIT CL

TREVAUNANCE CL

REVOSE CL

WHEAL

TREGEASE RD

BEACONSFIELD PLACE

QUAY LANE

QUAY ROAD

QUAY ROAD

WHEAL KITTY LA

GRENVILLE DR

IRENE DR

LAMBO

3285

STIPPY STAPPY

TOWN HILL

QUAY ROAD

ROSEMUNDY

WATER

ST. AGNES

CHURCHTOWN ROAD

CHEGWIN GDNS

WHITES CL

TRELANGWIN AV

BEACONSFIELD RD

Coastguard
Station

Shafts (disused)

KEMPS CL

TRELAWNEY

PENGARTH RD

BRITISH ROAD

CASTLE MEADOWS

ROSEMUNDY

GOONOWN ROAD

GOONOWN LA

POLBREAN AV

LAWRENCE RD

P RD

P

DURNING RD

DURNING RD

WHITWORTH CL

LAWRENCE RD

BOLSTER RD

POLBREAN RD

VICARAGE ROAD

PENWINNICK ROAD

PENWINNICK CL

Hotel

Cemetery

MIDDLEGATE

Goonown Farm

B3277

GOONVREA

Penwinnick
Farm

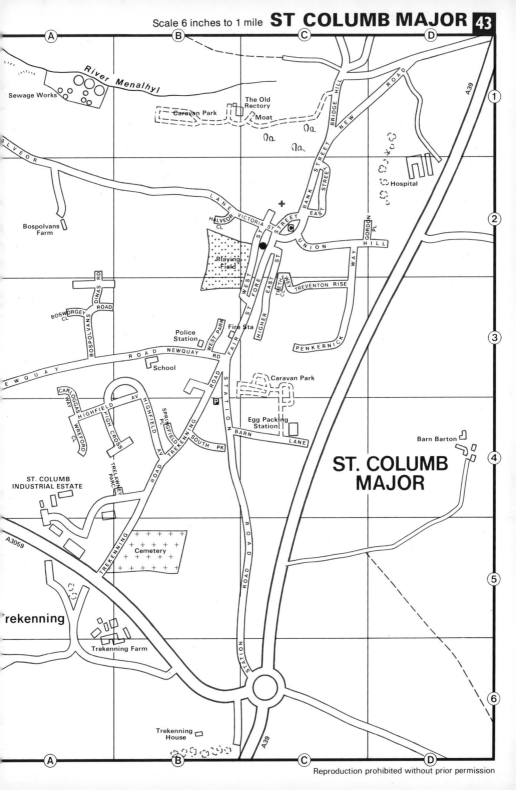

River Menalhyl

Sewage Works

The Old Rectory

Caravan Park

Moat

A39

BRIDGE HILL

NEW ROAD

STREET

BANK STREET

EAST STREET

Hospital

1

HALVEOR

HALVEOR LANE

VICTORIA

CL

Bospolvans Farm

GORDON PL

HILL

WAY

UNION

2

DINAS RD

ROAD

Playing Field

WEST ST

FORE ST

EAST ST

CRETH KEY

TREVENTON RISE

C

BOSWORGEY CL

BOSPOLVANS

Police Station

WEST PARK

Fire Sta

FAIR

HIGHER ST

PENKERNICK

3

ROAD NEWQUAY RD

School

NEWQUAY

CARLOGGAS WAY

HIGHFIELD

HIGH CROSS

HIGHFIELD AV

SPRINGFIELD

TREKENNING

ROAD

STATION

P

Caravan Park

4

WREFORD CL

AV

PL

SOUTH PK

BARN LANE

Egg Packing Station

Barn Barton

ST. COLUMB INDUSTRIAL ESTATE

TRELAWNEY PARK

ST. COLUMB MAJOR

A3059

Cemetery

TREKENNING

ROAD

5

rekenning

Trekenning Farm

STATION ROAD

6

Trekenning House

A39

B C D

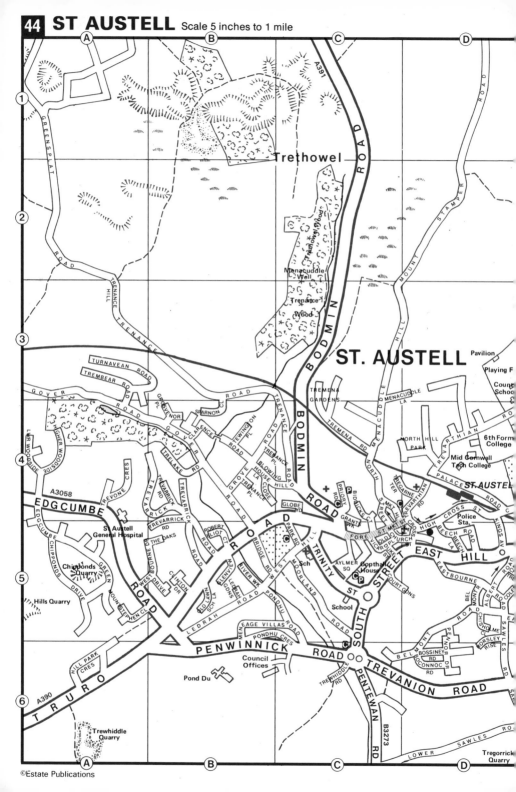

44 ST AUSTELL Scale 5 inches to 1 mile

Trethowel

Menacuddle Well

Trenance Wood

ST. AUSTELL

Pavilion

Playing F

Count
Schoo

TREMENA
GARDENS

MENACUDDLE
LA

TURNAVEAN ROAD

TREMBEAR ROAD

GOVER

ROAD

TRENANCE

HILL

NORTH HILL
PARK

6th Form
College

Mid Cornwall
Tech College

ST. AUSTEL

TREMENA RD

NORTH

ST. MNT.HI

TREVARTHIAN

PALACE

SPARNON

GROSVENOR PL

CLARENCE

RD

REWINGTON
ROAD

TRELAKE
RD

TREVARRICK

GOVER

TRENANCE

ROAD

BLOWING
HOUSE
HILL

TRENANCE
PL

GLOBE
YD

PRIORY
PK

GRANTS

TREGARNE

TER

BIDDICKS

CROSS

ST

Police
Sta.

REVONE CRES

HIGHER WOODSIDE

LWR WOODSIDE

TREVARRICK RD

TREVARRICK
CT

TRELAKE
RD

ROBERT
ELIOT
CT

GROVE

ROAD

GLENVIA GDNS

FORE

CHURCH

ST.MNT.HI

HIGH

BEECH

RD

BEECH

KINGS AV

A3058

EDGCUMBE

ST Austell
General Hospital

THE OAKS

CLINTON

RD

ROBERTS

ROAD

LEMON
RD

BRIDGE
ROAD

PARK RD

MOORLAND

TRINITY

ST

VICTORIA

ROPE

CHURCH

CROSS
ST

EAST

HILL

EASTBOURNE

BELL

MONT

ALBERT

ROAD

EDGCUMBE

CHIPPONDS

Chipponds
Quarry

WEST BOURNE DRIVE

GREEN

EDGCUMBE

RD

ROAD

NANPEAN
SCH LA

OLD VICARAGE

LEDRAH

RIVER WK

WEST

AYLMER
SQ

Sch

Copthall
House

COURT GDNS

ST

School

SOUTH

STREET

BELMONT

PENNOR DR

BOSSINEY
RD

CONNOC
RD

CHISHOLME
RD

HORSLEY
RD

RISE

Hills Quarry

MOUNT STEPHEN CL

DRIVE

LEDRAH

ROAD

MENEAGE VILLAS

PONDHU CRES

PONDHU

ROAD

PONDHU ROAD

Council
Offices

PENWINNICK

ROAD

TREWHIDDLE
RD

TRINITY
ROAD

PENTEWAN
RD

TREVANION

ROAD

B3273

HILL PARK
CRES

A390

TRURO

Pond Du

Trewhiddle
Quarry

LOWER

SAWLES

RD

Tregorrick
Quarry

©Estate Publications

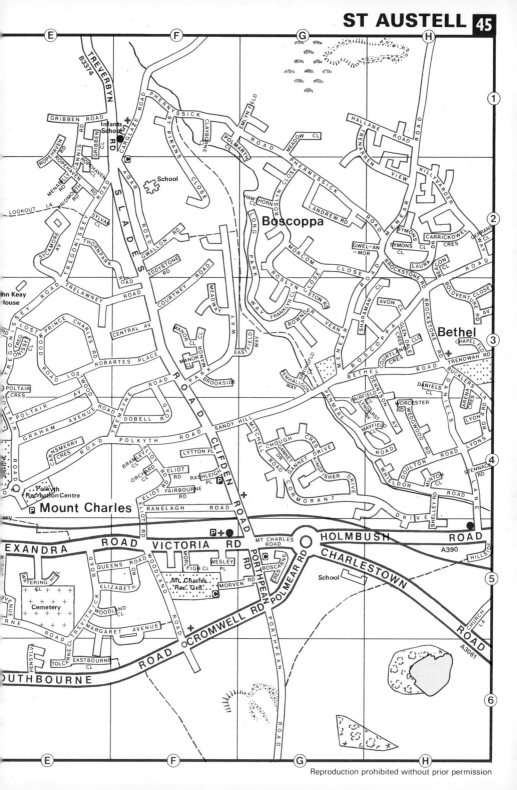

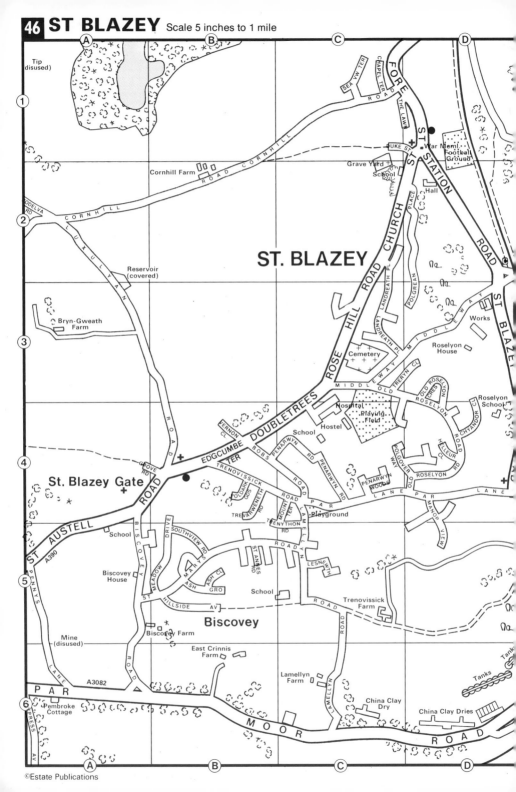

Ⓐ Ⓑ Ⓒ Ⓓ

① ② ③ ④ ⑤ ⑥

Tip (disused)

Cornhill Farm
CORNHILL ROAD
RODELVA RD
CORNHILL ROAD
LUXULYAN ROAD

Reservoir (covered)

Bryn-Gweath Farm

ST. BLAZEY

SEA VW TER
CHAPEL TER
THE LAWN
ROAD
FORE
ST STATION
DUKE ST
War Mem'l
Football Ground
Grave Yard
School
Hall
CHURCH ROAD
ST BLAZEY ROAD
PLACE
LANDREATH PL
POLGREAN
MIDDLE WAY
Works
Roselyon House
ROSE HILL ROAD
Cemetery
MIDDLE WAY
OLD TRERYN CL
OLD ROSELYON CRES
ROSELYON
Roselyon School
CHYANDOR CL
HELLEUR CL
ROSELYON ROAD
POLOVER WAY

DOUBLETREES
VERNON CL
TER
EDGCUMBE
GROVE RD
Hospital
Playing Field
School
Hostel
BOBS
PENARWIN RD
PENARWIN RD
POLDARK RD
TRENOVISSICK RD
TREVARWENETH RD
MOUNT TER
TRENYTHON RD
ROAD
LAMELLYN
PAR LANE
PENARWIN WOODS
MANOR VIEW
PAR LANE

St. Blazey Gate

ST AUSTELL ROAD
A390
PENNYS
School
BISCOVEY ROAD
SOUTHVIEW RD
MEADOW DRIVE
ST MARYS RD
ASH GRO
ASH CL
ST ANNES RD
Playground
ROAD
LESNCWTH
Biscovey House
HILLSIDE AV
School
Biscovey
ROAD
Trenovissick Farm

Mine (disused)
Biscovey Farm
East Crinnis Farm
PAR
A3082
ROAD
LANE
Pembroke Cottage
CYPRESS AV
Lamellyn Farm
LAMELLYN ROAD
China Clay Dry
Tanks
China Clay Dries
Tanks

MOOR ROAD

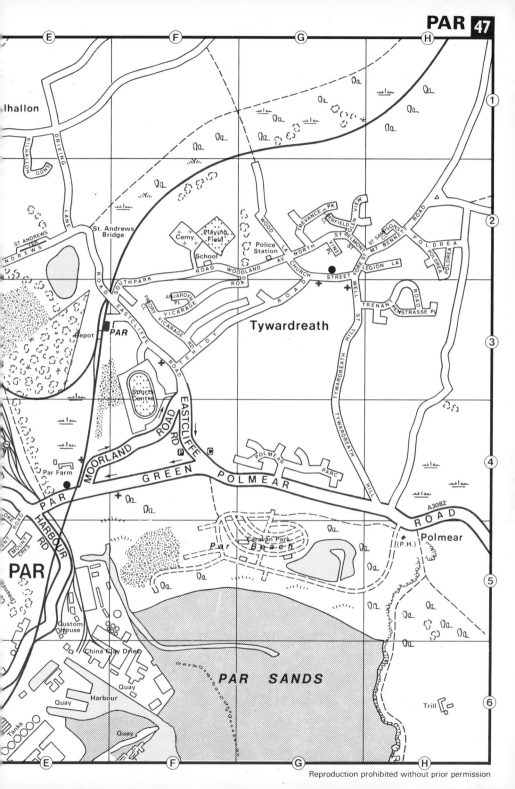

Ihallon

E F G H

1

St. Andrews
Bridge

St. Andrews

Cemy.
Playing
Field
School

Police
Station

Depot

PAR

Tywardreath

Sports
Centre

Par Farm

MOORLAND ROAD

EASTCLIFFE RD

GREEN POLMEAR

ROAD

POLMEAR
PARC

Polmear
(P.H.)

A3082

PAR

PAR HARBOUR RD

Custom
House

China Clay Dries

Par Beach

Caravan Park

Quay

Harbour

Quay

Tanks

Quay

PAR SANDS

Trill

2

3

4

5

6

KILHALLON DRIVING LANE
GDNS

SOUTHPARK ROAD
EASTCLIFFE ROAD
PRIORY CL
VICARAGE RD
JARDYN PL
VICARAGE RD
HIDY

WOODLAND ROAD
ROP

WOOD LA
NORTH
AV CHURCH
ST
VINE PL

TREVANCE PK
FERFIELD
ST BELMONT
VIEW
FOREST ST
LEGION LA
WELL ST
TRENAN
PENSTRASSE PL
ROAD

ST SAMPSONS CL
MT BENNET
POLDREA
POLDREA

TYWARDREATH HILL
TYWARDREATH HILL

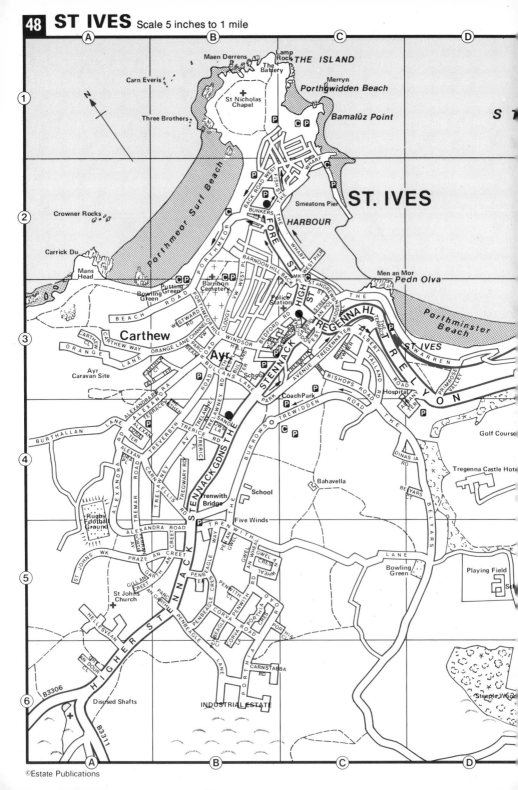

THE ISLAND

Maen Derrens
Lamp Rock
The Battery
Carn Everis
Merryn
Porthgwidden Beach
St Nicholas Chapel
Bamalūz Point
Three Brothers

ST. IVES

Smeatons Pier
HARBOUR

Crowner Rocks

BUNKERS HILL

Carrick Du

Mans Head

Men an Mor
Pedn Olva

Porthmeor Surf Beach

Porthminster Beach

Bowling Green
Putting Green

Barnoon Cemetery

Police Station

ST IVES
WARREN

BEACH ROAD

Carthew

Orange Lane

Ayr

Ayr Caravan Site

School

TREGENNA HL

Hospital

BURTHALLAN LANE

Coach Park

BISHOPS ROAD

Golf Course

Tregenna Castle Hotel

BELYARS

DINAS IA RD

Rugby Football Ground

STENNACK GDNS THE

Bahavella

School

Trenwith Bridge

Five Winds

Playing Field

Bowling Green

St Johns Church

PRAZE AN CREET

PENBEAGLE

PENWITH

GWEL

CARNSTABBA RD

Steeple Wood

B3306

Disused Shafts

B3311

INDUSTRIAL ESTATE

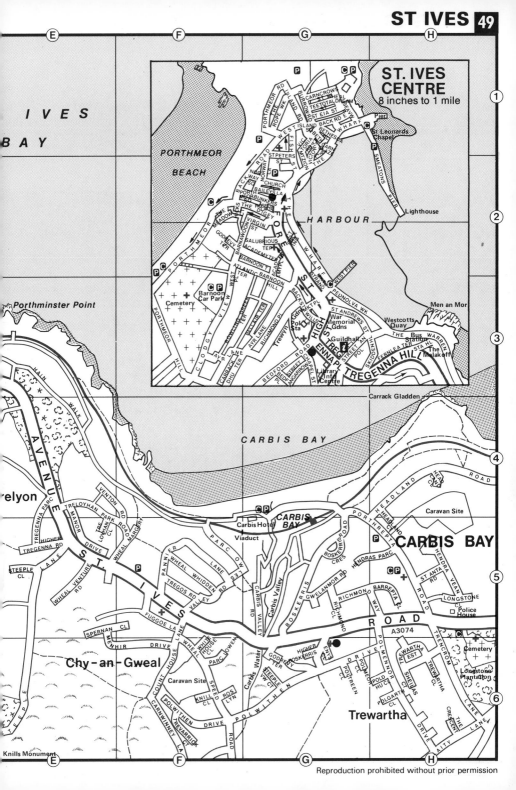

ST. IVES
CENTRE
8 inches to 1 mile

IVES
BAY

PORTHMEOR
BEACH

HARBOUR

Lighthouse

St Leonards Chapel
Pier

Men an Mor

Westcotts Quay

Bus Station
The Malakoff

Porthminster Point

Barnoon Car Park
Cemetery

War Memorial Gdns
St Andrews St
Guildhall
Library Info Centre

TREGENNA HILL

Carrack Gladden

CARBIS BAY

Carbis Hotel
Viaduct

CARBIS BAY

Caravan Site

ST IVES

elyon

Chy - an - Gweal

Caravan Site

Police House

Cemetery
Longstone Plantation

A3074

Trewartha

Knills Monument

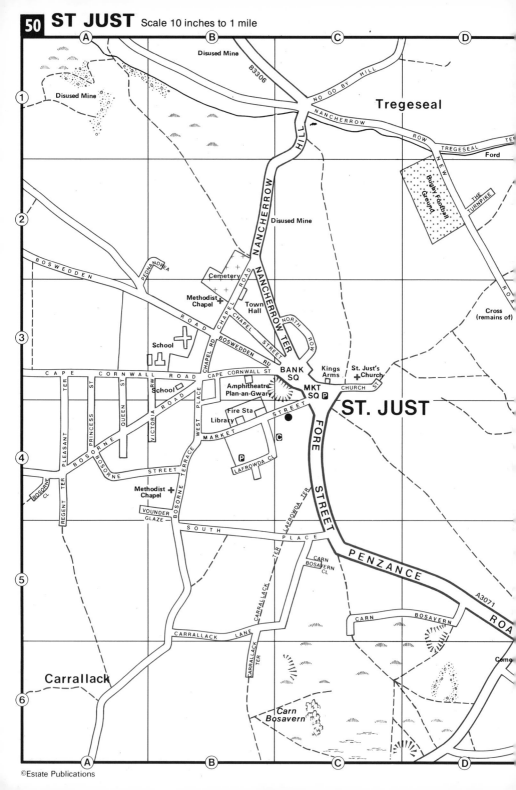

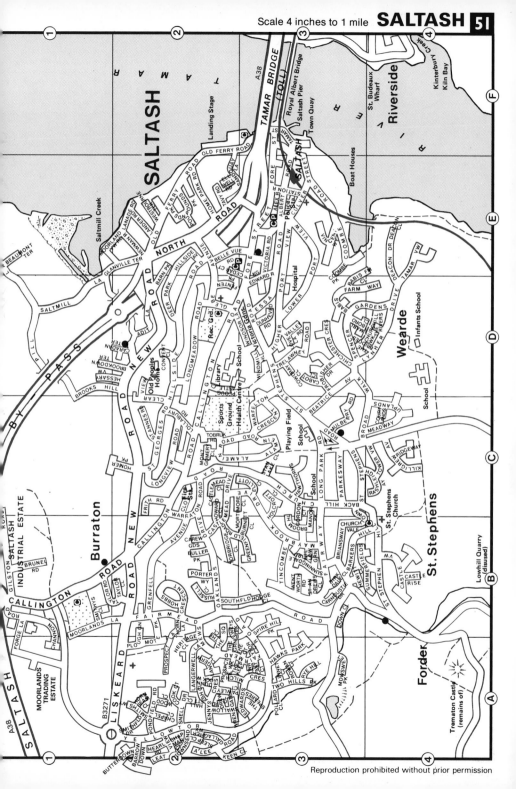

Ford
Boscolleth Mill
Penhaldarva House
Caravan Park
Pencoo Farm
B3284
NEW MILLS LANE
Ford
COOSEBEAN
River Kenwyn
COMP
Treliske Preparatory School
TRELISKE IND. EST.
TRELISKE HOSPITAL
OAK LA
A390
PENVENTINNE LANE
Golf Course
TRELISKE LANE
BARTON MEADOW LANE
BOSVEAN GARDENS
VIGO
BOS
TRESAWLS ROAD
GLOWETH VW
TRESAWLS AV
LAMELLYN DRIVE
CRYON VW
NANSAVALLON RD
TREVEAN RD
PENWERRIS LA
ST THOMAS
TRELISKE LANE
MALABAR
CORNISHO CL
ASC
TRE BED
BENHENNA
CALD LAND RD
HAR COUR
CRESCENT
CRESCENT
ALMA CRES
SCHOOL
School
HILL CREST
SUNNINGDALE
STATION ROAD
TRURO
ROAD
THE C
CRES GDNS
AVONDALE
Library
Fire Sta.
O ROAD
HIGHERTOWN
PROCARD CL
ALBANY ROAD
KIRBY RD
FERNE CL
DOBBS
Council Offices
School
School
+ School
DUDMAN DR
KENNA PK
KESTLE
VALLEY GRO
DUDMAN RD
LANE
TREVEYER WAY
VALLEY VIEW
VALLEY DR
TRAFFINE ROAD
EVEA CL
NEWBRIDGE WAY
RETHOWAN HEIGHTS
Penwithers Junction
PENWETHER
TREDEW
ROAD
COLD
CHA
County Hall
Football Ground
Nansavallan Wood

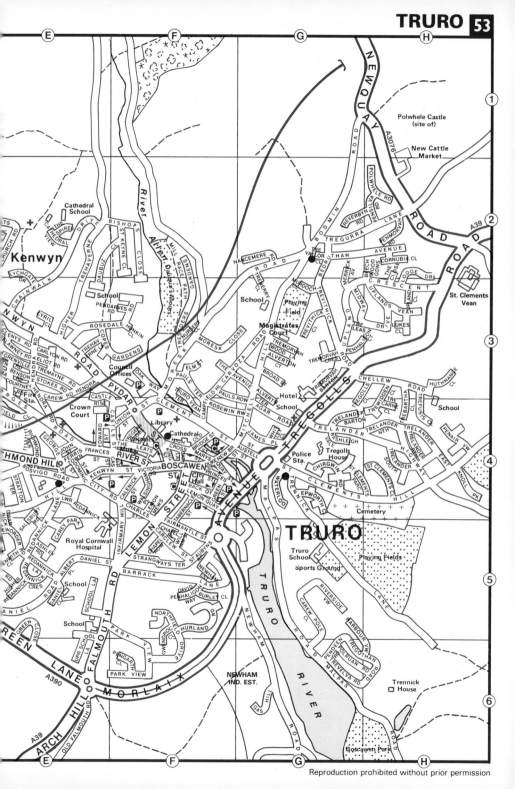

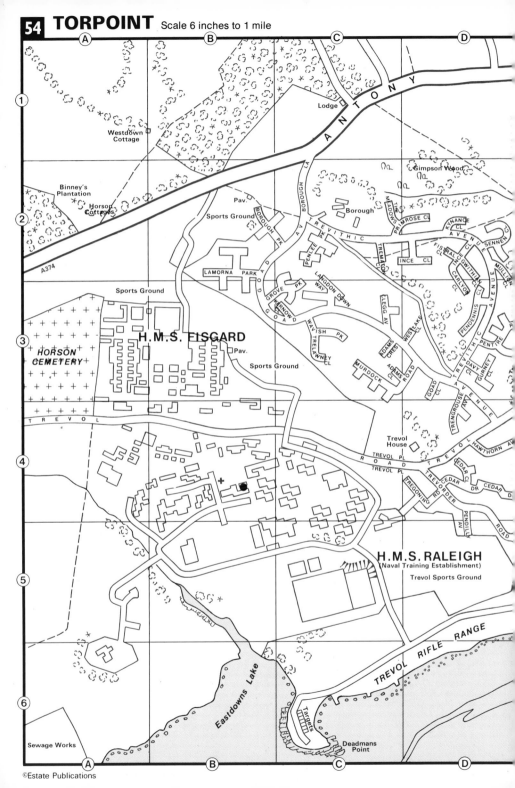

A B C D

1

Lodge

Westdown
Cottage

A N T O N Y

Gimpson Wood

Binney's
Plantation

Pav.
Sports Ground

Borough

2 Horson
Cottages

THE MEADOWS

PRIMROSE CL

KINANCE CL

AVENUE

SENNEN CL

A374

BOROUGH LA

BOROUGH PK

TREVITHIC

TREMATON CL

INCE CL

FISTRAL CL

LOWITHIC CL

MULLION

Sports Ground

LAMORNA PARK

GROVE RD

PENLEE

KERNOW CL

GROVE PK

LANGDON DOWN

WAY

WAVISH PK

ELEGG AV

WESTLAKE

CARLYON CL

PENDENNIS

PENTIRE

MULLION AVENUE

3 HORSON
CEMETERY

H.M.S. FISGARD

Pav.

TRELAWNEY CL

ADAMS CRES

MURDOCK

ADAMS ROAD

GOLD CL

REITH AVENUE

DAVY CL

GURNEY CL

Sports Ground

TREVOL

Trevol
House

TRENGROUSE AV

4 Trevol PL

ROAD

TREVOL PL

TREVOL

TREVORDER ROAD

CEDAR GR

HAWTHORN AV

CEDAR DR

TREGONING

PENDILLY AV

CEDAR CL

ROAD

H.M.S. RALEIGH
(Naval Training Establishment)

5 Trevol Sports Ground

TREVOL RIFLE RANGE

Eastdowns Lake

6

Targets

Sewage Works

Deadmans
Point

A B C D

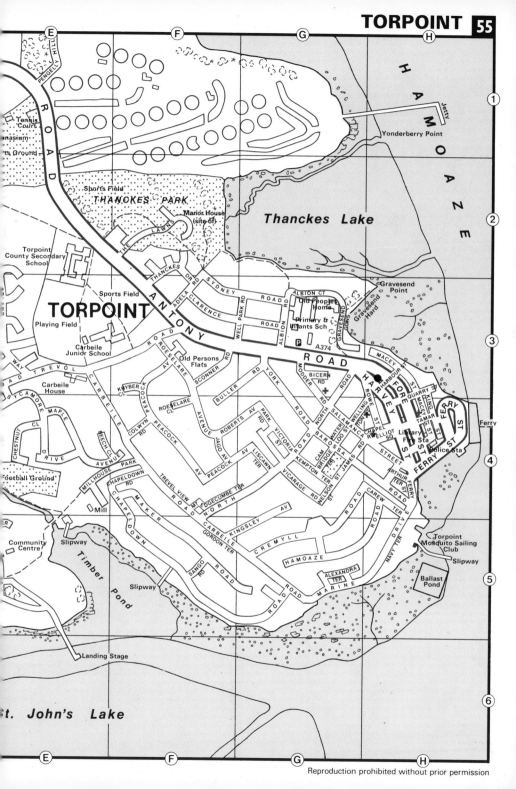

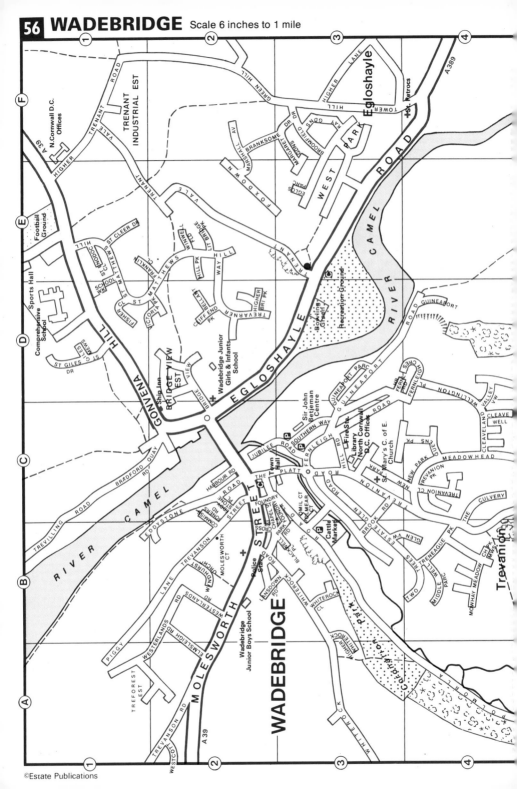